TAKING ITS LEAD FROM TOP
DESIGNERS AND THE CATWALK

101 ways to customize your clothes

using beading, trimming, printing, dyeing,
appliqué and embroidery

Petra Boase

CARLTON
BOOKS

To Mum, Dad and Marc

THIS IS A CARLTON BOOK

Text, design and special photography copyright
© 2001 Carlton Books Limited

Reprinted in 2008.

This edition published by Carlton Books Limited
20 Mortimer Street, London W1T 3JW

A CIP catalogue record for this book is available from
the British Library

ISBN 978 1 84222 329 1

Printed and bound in Italy

Editorial Manager: Venetia Penfold
Art Director: Penny Stock
Commissioning Editor: Zia Mattocks
Writer/Editor: Lisa Dyer
Designer: Nigel Soper
Photographer: Lucy Pope
Stylists: Petra Boase and Jane McAllister
Production Controller: Janette Davis

Neither the authors nor the publisher can accept
responsibility for any accident, injury or damage that
results from using the ideas, information or advice
offered in this book.

Contents

1

Ribbons, Trimmings & Feathers

Velvet, lace, feather, fur, fringe or sequin trimmings, all in different styles and textures, can be used to transform an item of clothing in a flash. Available from haberdashery departments and sewing stores, trims can inspire different effects. Lace adds instant romance; sequin or beaded trim with feathers is street-stylish and contemporary; and piping or rickrack gives a girly sweetness to outfits.

Pink Piped
Tuxedo
Trousers

REVISIT THE 1970S DANCE FLOOR with these tuxedo-styled piped trousers. The tougher, more masculine image of tuxedos is married with shiny satin for a real disco babe feel, making the trousers the perfect partywear for girls who hate skirts. This customizing idea would also work well for daywear by adding satin piping to the seams of jeans, chinos or pencil skirts.

WHAT YOU NEED
• Black satin trousers
• Tape measure
• Pale pink satin cord
• Scissors
• Pins
• Pale pink sewing thread

HOW TO DO IT

1 Place the trousers on a flat work surface and measure the side seam. Cut two lengths of pink cord to size, adding an extra 15 mm ($^5/_8$ in) to each length.

2 Starting at the top of one trouser side seam, turn under the end of the cord by 5 mm ($^1/_4$ in) and pin it to abut the bottom of the waistband. Hand-sew it in place with a few couching stitches (see page 143).

3 Continue stitching the cord along the length of the seam with couching stitches. At the bottom of the trouser leg, turn the excess cord to the inside of the hem and stitch in place.

4 Repeat steps 2 and 3 to stitch the piping onto the side seam of the other trouser leg.

Fake Fur
Cardigan

FAKE FUR ADDS a Zsa Zsa Gabor touch to clothing, transporting the most standard item into the high-glamour end of fashion. Whether you want to pretend you are an up-and-coming starlet or just like the way fur frames the face, fake fur collars add luxe to a look. Attachable fur collars can be bought in different colours and sizes from sewing shops or notion stores; choose one that works with the collar on your cardigan.

WHAT YOU NEED
- Black cardigan with collar
- Brown fake fur attachable collar
- Pins
- Brown sewing thread
- Scissors
- Sewing needle

HOW TO DO IT
Pin the fake fur collar onto the right side of the cardigan collar. Hand-sew the collar in place along all edges using slipstitches and the brown thread (see page 143).

Leopard-print Trousers

TAKE A WALK ON THE WILD SIDE with leopard-print trousers. Top-to-toe animal prints are usually best reserved for the ghetto-fabulous and famous – or an It girl on a paparazzi-popping night out, but you can still take part in the trend with the more subtle approach here. Trimming sugar pink trousers with a leopard-print shows a lively attention-seeking attitude, but if you are fearful of heart, go more subtle by using black trousers.

WHAT YOU NEED
- Pink trousers
- Tape measure
- Scissors
- 5 cm- (2 in-) wide iron-on leopard-print hem tape
- Pins
- Iron and ironing board

HOW TO DO IT
1 Measure the trouser hem. Cut two lengths of leopard-print tape to size, adding an extra 15 mm ($^5/_8$ in) to each.

2 Starting at the inside seam, pin each length of tape to a trouser leg, abutting the hem edge of the trousers. At the join, turn under the raw edge on one short end and neatly overlap onto the other end.

3 Place the trousers on an ironing or sleeve board and fuse one leg at a time. Following the manufacturer's instructions, cover the tape with a damp cloth and iron in place, removing the pins in each section as you work.

Flower & Feather
Corsage

SHOULDERS ARE THE NEW erogenous zone to be tapped in the fashion stakes, and nothing makes a sexier silhouette than a one-shoulder top. The asymmetrical off-the-shoulder look is contemporary and provocative, especially when embellished with a shocking pink corsage. Flowers have always denoted sexuality, and fake flower corsages give an immediate allure, drawing attention to the face, breast, shoulder, waist or wherever you place them.

WHAT YOU NEED

- Pink feathers
- Pink fabric flower
- Pink sewing thread
- Sewing needle
- Scissors
- Large blank brooch pin
- Black stretchy one-shoulder top

HOW TO DO IT

1 Arrange the feathers in your hands and trim the quills to size. Here the feathers measure 15 cm (6 in) in height. Bind the end of the quills by wrapping them with thread and knotting firmly.

2 Hand-sew the plumage onto the back of the fabric flower, using overhand stitches (see page 143).

3 Hand-sew a brooch pin onto the back of the flower. To make the first knot, run the thread through one hole in the pin and into the flower, leaving an extra 'tail' of thread hanging. Knot the thread tightly to the hanging end, and then continue to stitch, wrapping the thread through the brooch pin and flower as you work. Knot to the previous stitches to secure. Repeat the procedure to secure the flower to the pin through the second hole.

4 Pin the corsage onto the shoulder of the black top.

Glittery Pink
Flower Top

WHAT YOU NEED
· Pink glittery v-necked top
· Pink fabric flower
· Pink sewing thread
· Sewing needle

HOW TO DO IT
Holding the flower firmly in place on the centre 'v' of the neckline, slipstitch it to the top, working underneath the flower (see page 143).

Pink Rosebuds

Get into the baby doll trend with puffy sleeves and a candy pink sweetbriar neckline. Dress it down to keep the look fresh and modern. Frilly feminine tops always look more chic-meets-street when paired with some dirty-and-lowdown denim jeans.

WHAT YOU NEED
- About 100 pink ribbon rosebuds
- Scissors
- Pink round-neck top
- Pink sewing thread
- Sewing needle

HOW TO DO IT

1 If your pink ribbon roses have green ribbon loops sewn on the reverse side (for leaves), remove them by snipping the attaching thread.

2 Starting on one shoulder seam, hand-sew a rosebud along the neckline edge of the top, using a few slip-stitches to secure it in place. Continue stitching on more roses, working around the inner edge of the neckline to the other shoulder seam, and stitching them as closely together as possible.

3 When you have completed the first row, repeat step 2 to stitch a second row of roses just outside the first.

Velvet & Rosebuds

UPDATE A PLAIN TOP with velvet and roses and make the everyday into the special occasion. This is for moments when you want to show your soft side. Paired with the right accessories and a skirt, the top can go from a wedding reception to a hot date, or anywhere in between. A plain strappy velvet top was used here to layer the two tones of green velvet, but you can choose a cotton or Lycra-mix version if you prefer.

WHAT YOU NEED

- Green velvet strappy top or camisole
- Tape measure
- Blue-green velvet trim
- Pins
- Blue-green and red sewing thread
- Sewing needle
- Scissors
- 7 red ribbon rosebuds

Tip

Use this trim idea along the hem of a skirt or a sweater to add romance. Roses can be stitched almost anywhere – into lace trims, onto sleeve cuffs or along the front opening of a pretty pastel cardigan.

HOW TO DO IT

1 Place the top on a flat work surface. Measure the length of the front neckline between the straps. Cut a length of velvet trim to size, adding an extra 1 cm (½ in) for folding under the short ends.

2 Pin the trim flush to the neckline, folding under 5 mm (¼ in) at each short end. Hand-sew the ribbon in place along both long sides using a slipstitch and the blue-green thread (see page 143). Remove the pins.

3 At approximately 2 cm (¾ in) intervals, hand-sew the ribbon rosebuds onto the velvet trim using a tiny slipstitch and the red thread.

Feather
& Velvet Jeans

T HE FEATHER TREND shows no signs of abating. Frills of feathers lend an ultra-fashionable look to clothes, which can be decadent and hip or invoke movie-star glamour from a bygone era. Taking inspiration from those Gucci jeans several years back, these feather-trimmed jeans belong to the first category by claiming a rock-chick cool. The feather-cuffed sweater, on the other hand, gives a feeling of retro luxe – anyone sporting these sleeves would certainly not be expected to wash dishes.

WHAT YOU NEED
- Jeans
- Tape measure
- Red feather trim
- 15 mm ($^5/_8$ in) wide red velvet ribbon
- Scissors
- Pins
- Sewing machine
- Red sewing thread

Feather-cuffed
Sweater

WHAT YOU NEED
- Black woollen or cotton sweater
- Ribbon-banded feather trim
- Pins
- Cotton thread the colour of the sweater
- Sewing needle
- Scissors
- Tape measure

HOW TO DO IT

1 Measure around the sweater cuffs. Cut two lengths of ribbon-banded feather trim to size, adding an extra 3 cm (1¼ in) onto each.

2 Turn the sweater wrong sides out. Starting at the seam of each cuff, pin the feather trim along the edge of the cuff, overlapping neatly at the seam to join.

3 Hand-sew the trim in place, through the edge of the feather band, using a slipstitch (see page 143). Add a few extra stitches at the join to secure firmly. Remove the pins and turn the sweater right sides out.

HOW TO DO IT

1 Place the jeans on a flat work surface and measure the hem. Cut two lengths each of feather trim and velvet ribbon to size, adding an extra 1 cm (½ in) to each .

2 Pin a length of feather trim above the hem on the right side of each jeans legs so that the feathers rest along the bottom edge of the hem. Join the ends at the inside seam by neatly overlapping the trim.

3 Machine-stitch the trim in place on the right side of the jeans, using a straight stitch and red thread.

4 Add the velvet ribbon to both trouser legs. Pin the ribbon over the edge of the feather trim to conceal the stitching and ends. Join the ribbon ends at the inside seam by turning under one short end and overlapping it onto the other. Machine-stitch along both long sides of the ribbon using a straight stitch.

Tied Ribbon Top

THE DELICATE FADED COLOURS and comfy thermal of this top provide a fluid softness that is touchable and undeniably feminine. It is perfect for those times when you want to marry comfort with prettiness, whether you are cocooning at home or out-and-about on a warm spring day. A top with a lace-trimmed neckline is essential for adding the ribbon to the neckline.

WHAT YOU NEED

- Lilac thermal sleeveless top
- Blue sewing thread
- Sewing needle
- Scissors
- Small blue sequins
- Beading needle
- 7 mm (¼ in) wide pink velvet ribbon, about 80 cm (32 in) long
- Bodkin or large-eye needle

HOW TO DO IT

1 Place the thermal top on a flat work surface, front side up. Using the pattern of the weave as a guide, hand-sew vertical lines of backstitch up the front of the top with blue sewing thread. Here five equally spaced lines were made, each one varying in length.

2 Hand-sew one or two small blue sequins every 4 cm (1½ in) up each vertical line. To do this, first make a knot on the wrong side and bring the thread through to the front. Thread through the hole in the sequin, and then insert the needle through the top, as close to the sequin as possible, but on the outside edge. Repeat again, anchoring the next stitch at opposite side of the sequin.

3 Thread the bodkin or large-eye needle with the velvet ribbon. Starting in the centre front of the top, evenly weave the ribbon in and out of gaps in the lace around the neckline. Tie the ends of ribbon in a bow.

Purple-trimmed Black Linen Dress

CLEAN LINES ARE ENHANCED by a purple border, adding a certain preppy poise and pared-down good taste to a simple black linen dress. Classy and ladylike, the dress cries out for a summer garden party or a day at the races or the regatta. Any other colours of binding could be used; try edging the dress in white for that crisper, more cutting edge, black-and-white effect seen on the catwalk.

WHAT YOU NEED

- Black linen dress
- Tape measure
- 2 cm- (¾ in-) wide purple satin bias binding
- Scissors
- Sewing machine
- Pins
- Sewing needle
- Tacking (basting) thread in a contrasting colour
- Purple sewing thread
- 30 cm (12 in) black cord
- Black thread

HOW TO DO IT

1 Adapt the measurements for the bias binding you need according to the design of your dress. Cut out lengths of bias binding to size, adding an extra 1 cm (½ in) onto each length. For the dress shown here, five lengths of binding were cut: one length for around the neckline; two lengths for the side sections of the dress; and two more for the back zip-to-side sections.

2 Starting at the back of the dress where the zip starts, insert the top of the dress into the seam of the folded binding, making sure that the raw edges of the binding are tucked under. Pin in place, and repeat to pin the bias binding lengths onto the other back zip-to-side seam edge, onto the sides and around the neckline. At each join, turn under one short end of the binding and overlap it on top of the other raw end.

3 Tack (baste) through both sides of the binding all round the dress to hold the binding in place.

4 Working on the right side of the dress, machine-stitch the binding in place using a straight stitch and the purple thread. Remove the tacking (basting) stitches.

5 Cut the black cord in half and tie each half in a bow. Using the black thread, slipstitch the bows onto the dress straps at the bias binding ends (see page 143).

Raspberry
Ribbon & Bead Cardigan

THE PLAINEST CARDIGAN can be jazzed up with frilly trim and beading to give a new romantic look. The top makes a warm wrap for floaty dresses or strappy camisoles, whether it is keeping shoulders warm in nippy weather or in ice-cold air conditioning. For a lively flash of colour peeking from the neckline, use a juicy lime or zesty lemon trim.

WHAT YOU NEED

- Raspberry-coloured cotton cardigan
- Tape measure
- 1 cm- (½ in-) wide ribbon frill trim, with the frill measuring 5 mm (¼ in) deep
- Scissors
- Pins
- Tacking (basting) thread in a contrasting colour
- Sewing needle
- Red thread
- 1 container (about 400) small red beads
- Beading needle

HOW TO DO IT

1 Measure the cardigan to work out how much ribbon you will need. Measure along the front opening from the bottom hem, round the neckline and down the length of the inner front opening. To this measurement, add 1 cm (½ in) for turning under the short ribbon ends.

2 Cut the ribbon to size and pin it to the wrong side of the cardigan along the front opening edges and the neckline. Turn under the short raw ends at the hem.

3 Tack (baste) the ribbon frill in place. Hand-sew the ribbon along the edges and neckline of the cardigan using tiny hidden slipstitches and the red thread (see page 143). Remove the tacking (basting) stitches.

4 Using a beading needle and red thread, sew small beads randomly along the front-opening panel and neckline. Sew each bead on separately, making two stitches through each one, and knotting securely.

Raffia-trimmed Skirt

Shake your bon-bon à la Ricky Martin with a back-fringed skirt in hot pink. Get the Latino vibe pumping by mixing the skirt with a slinky top and flamenco dancing shoes, and hit the salsa clubs. Alternatively, go all country and cowgirl by working suede or leather fringing onto a denim skirt.

WHAT YOU NEED
- Pink cotton skirt
- Black raffia fringe trim
- Pins
- Black thread
- 14-20 round metal studs
- Sewing machine
- Pins
- Scissors
- Tape measure

HOW TO DO IT

1 Place the skirt on a flat work surface, back side up. Measure the back of the skirt where you want the raffia fringe. Here the fringing goes fully side seam to side seam and it is positioned at a slight 'v' curve, about 10 cm (4 in) from the waist at the deepest point.

2 Cut the raffia fringe trim to the back measurement, adding an extra 1 cm (½ in) for folding under the ends.

3 Fold under and pin both short ends of the trim by 5 mm (¼ in). Pin the fringing in place on the skirt, curving slightly at the centre point to create the 'v'. Measure to ensure that the trim is equidistant from the waistband on both sides and the 'v' falls in the centre.

4 Machine-stitch the trim in place on the right side, about 5 mm (¼ in) from the top edge of the raffia.

5 Insert the metal studs into the edge of the raffia, making sure they are equally spaced apart. Working one at a time and following the manufacturer's instructions, press the first stud firmly into the raffia from the right side. On the reverse side of the skirt, bend back the prongs to secure the stud.

Fluffy
Maribou Top

ANY VA-VA VOOM PARTY GIRL will have an instant affinity for these come-hither bedroom looks that spell non-stop action. The trims are playful, conjuring up images of a silver screen siren sipping a martini while lounging seductively in a swanky boudoir or jazz club. These two customizing designs will be sure to bring out the Mae West bad-girl in you.

WHAT YOU NEED
· Black strappy top
· Tape measure
· Scissors
· Pale blue maribou trim
· Pins
· Pale blue sewing thread
· Sewing needle

HOW TO DO IT

1 Place the black top on a flat work surface. Measure the straps and cut two lengths of maribou trim to size, adding an extra 1 cm (½ in) to each length. Measure along the top edge of the top and cut a length of maribou trim to size, adding an extra 1 cm (½ in).

2 Pin the maribou trim to the straps and hand-sew in place along both long sides, using slipstitches through the back of the trim (see page 143). Remove the pins.

3 Starting at one side seam, pin maribou trim around the top edge, turning under neatly at the join and concealing the trim ends of the straps. Hand-sew the maribou trim in place along the top edge, using small slipstitches, and then remove the pins.

Pink Fluoro Feathers

WHAT YOU NEED
· Sewing machine
· Pins
· 10 pink feathers
· Pink fluorescent sleeveless top
· Pink thread
· Scissors

HOW TO DO IT

Pin the quill of each feather 5 mm (¼ in) in from the neckline of the top and 2 cm (¾ in) apart, from shoulder seam to shoulder seam only. Machine-stitch the feathers 15 mm (⅝ in) in from the end of the quills using a straight stitch. Trim the quill ends.

Rickrack camisole

LINGERIE GETS OUT OF the bedroom with this charming rickrack trim. The black borders draw attention to the bustline, keeping the look sexy but sweet. Adding the black trim to different colours of camisole allows tops to be mixed with all those black basics in your wardrobe, thus extending the range of outfits on offer. The camisole looks especially good when worn under a tailored black trouser suit, giving a hint of seductiveness to power dressing.

WHAT YOU NEED

- Pink camisole
- Tape measure
- Wide and narrow black rickrack
- Scissors
- Sewing machine
- Pins
- Black thread
- Sewing needle (optional)

Tip

For a different, more casual, effect, stitch rows of coloured rickrack trim next to each other to create a multicoloured striped effect that will work well on T-shirts, along the hem of jeans or on denim handbags.

HOW TO DO IT

1 Place the camisole on a flat work surface. You will need four lengths of rickrack to cover this top, but adjust the amount you need according to the design.

2 Measure across the bottom bustline and cut a wide length of rickrack to size, adding 1 cm (½ in) for turning under the ends. Measure the top edge of the camisole, from the straps to the sides and across the back, and cut a length of narrow rickrack to size, plus 1 cm (½ in). Measure the v-neck, from the straps to the deep 'v', and cut two lengths of rickrack to size, plus 1 cm (½ in); here the neckline is overlapped, so one piece of rickrack is longer than the other piece.

3 Starting at one side seam, pin the wide rickrack to the bustline seam, turning under the short ends by 5 mm (¼ in), Machine-stitch the rickrack in place along the centre of the trim, using a straight stitch. Alternatively, hand-sew in place with a running stitch.

4 Repeat step 3 to attach the narrow rickrack to the top edge and 'v' neckline of the camisole, aligning the rickrack with the edge of the camisole. Where each length joins, turn under one short end and overlap it onto the other end to make a neat finish.

Pleated Ribbon Camisole

ADD THE HAUTE COUTURE touch in the form of pleats to make a versatile camisole. Wear it demure and high-class, in Audrey Hepburn mode, or downright trashy and over the top. Teamed with satin black trousers or a jet-beaded skirt, the top goes cocktail; pair it with a thigh-high-slashed skirt, and it says pure sex appeal.

WHAT YOU NEED

- Black camisole
- Tape measure
- Ready-pleated ribbon trim
- Black sequin trim
- Scissors
- Pins
- Black thread
- Sewing needle

HOW TO DO IT

1 Place the camisole on a flat work surface and measure the entire way round the top edge. Cut a length of both ribbon and sequin trims to size, adding an extra 1 cm (½ in) to each for joining ends.

2 Starting at one of the side seams, pin the pleated ribbon around the top edge of the camisole. Where the two ends meet, fold under one of the short ends and overlap it onto the other end. Hand-sew the ribbon in place along the top edge, using a running stitch and the black thread. At the overlapped edge, sew a few extra slipstitches to secure the join. Remove the pins.

3 Starting at the same side seam, pin the sequin trim along the edge of the pleated ribbon, close to the edge of the neckline. To join the ends, overlap the short edges neatly. Hand-sew in place using a running stitch, following the centre machined stitching in the trim. Secure the overlapped ends with a few slipstitches. Remove the pins.

2

Beading, Sequins & Studs

The jewel-like quality of sequins, gemstones, beads and studs gives clothes a glamorous and exciting edge. A hem or seam can be decorated with diamantés or beads; a pocket or lapel can be punctuated by a few studs; or an entire garment can be worked to create an ornate piece. Take care when washing garments that are embellished and avoid ironing over sequins, as they will melt.

Turquoise Indian Mirror Top

ORNATE MIRROR SEQUINS GIVE clothes an exotic feel, and any colour combination can be used. Multicoloured sequins work well on a range of colours, but using the same colour gives a more subtle effect. You only need a few of these large embellished sequins to create maximum impact.

WHAT YOU NEED
- Turquoise sleeveless top
- 14-16 Indian mirror sequins (28-32 if you are decorating the back)
- Chalk or pen fabric marker
- Turquoise thread
- Scissors
- Sewing needle

HOW TO DO IT

1 Place the top on a flat surface and arrange the sequins until you are happy with the overall design. Here, three sequins were placed along the ribbed bottom edge and the others were spaced randomly.

2 With the chalk or fabric pen, mark a dot at the point where you want to position each mirrored sequin. Repeat on the back of the top, if desired.

3 Hand-sew the mirror sequins to the top at the marked positions and using the turquoise thread. To do this, knot the thread and, holding the sequin in place, bring the thread through the embroidered edge of the sequin from the reverse side of the top. Anchor with a small straight stitch. Continue making stitches around the edge of the sequin to secure it in place. If you like, pin each sequin in place to help hold it while you sew. Repeat to attach all the sequins.

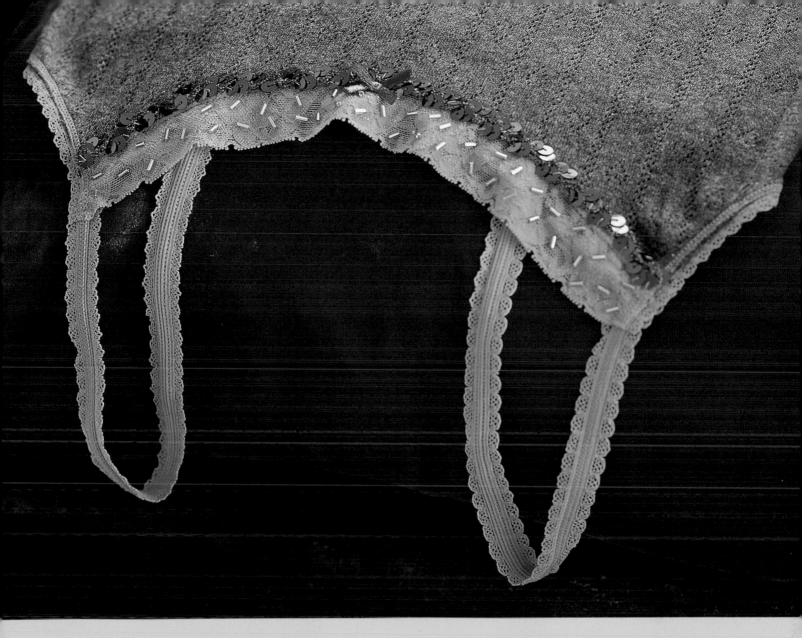

Sequinned Thermal Camisole

TAKE A BASIC CHAIN-STORE camisole top, available in a wide range of colours, and make it more upbeat by adding a dainty detailing of sequin trim and beads in a colour that complements the lace trim. No one will ever be able to tell that your inexpensive DIY version hasn't come from the trendiest boutique.

WHAT YOU NEED

- Grey lace-trimmed camisole with pink bow
- Tape measure
- Turquoise sequin trim
- Scissors
- Pins
- Turquoise and pink thread
- Sewing needle
- About 50 turquoise glass bugle beads, measuring 5 mm (¼ in) long
- Beading needle

HOW TO DO IT

1 Measure along the neckline of the camisole, just under the lace trim. Cut a length of sequin trim to size, plus 1 cm (½ in) extra.

2 Pin the sequin trim along the edge of the lace, turning under the raw ends at each side seam. If the trim is bulky, simply cut the ends flush with the side seam. Hand-sew the trim in place with slipstitches.

3 Using the beading needle, hand-sew the turquoise beads onto the lace trim at different angles for a 'scattered' look. Sew two stitches through each bead and knot on the wrong side of the camisole.

1 Draw the wings-and-heart design freehand onto the cardboard or paper and cut it out to make a template. Here the width from wingtip to wingtip is 31cm (12in), and the measurement from the top to the bottom of the heart is 14 cm (5 ½ in).

2 Place the top on a flat work surface, with the back side facing up, and position the cardboard or paper template on the shirt. Measure to make sure the design is centred, straight and about 10 cm (4 in) from the neckline. Draw round the template with the fabric marker. Lift off the template and draw in the lines for the sides of the heart with the marker.

3 Lay out the studs on the design to make sure you have a sufficient amount to go around. If desired, mark out the positions for the studs with the fabric marker so they are all evenly spaced. Here the large round studs were used for the wings and the star studs were used for the heart to add extra definition to the design.

4 Beginning with the heart, insert one stud at a time around the marked-out design. Following the manufacturer's instructions, firmly press a stud into the fabric. On the reverse side of the sweatshirt, bend back the prongs with your finger or a metal spoon to secure the stud. Continue the process to insert all the studs and complete the wings.

Studded Heart
Sweatshirt

FOR URBAN COOL WITH ATTITUDE, give your zip-up tops and polar fleeces a streetwise edge by adding studs. You can get that hardcore rock-chick look without ever having been on a Harley. Just combine the top with a hip-slung studded belt, down-and-dirty jeans and clunky boots.

WHAT YOU NEED

- Zip-up top in thick cotton jersey or sweatshirt material
- Cardboard or paper and a pen
- Scissors
- Tape measure
- Pins (if using a paper template)
- Black sweatshirt top
- 'Invisible' or 'fade away' pen fabric marker
- 52 large gold studs for wings
- 26 silver star studs for the heart

Studded Collar Zip-up

HOW TO DO IT

Using the neck seam of the top as a guideline, mark the points where you want to position the studs with the chalk or pen fabric marker. Here, three rows of studs have been used on each side of the collar and across the back collar. Insert the studs as described in step 4 of Studded Heart Sweatshirt, opposite.

WHAT YOU NEED

· Zip-up top with a high-neck collar in thick cotton jersey or sweatshirt material
· Chalk or pen fabric marker
· Tape measure
· About 100 round studs

Velvet Button Skirt

SOMETIMES THE PRETTIEST embellishment is the easiest. Why pay a small fortune for a designer skirt trimmed in buttons, when it is so simple to create one yourself? The lustrous shell buttons beautifully highlight the sheen of the velvet and accentuate the soft, feminine look.

WHAT YOU NEED

- Pale mauve velvet skirt
- Shell or mother-of-pearl buttons, enough for the hem
- Tape measure
- Cream-coloured thread
- Scissors
- Sewing needle

HOW TO DO IT

1 First make sure you have enough buttons to go the entire way round the hem of the skirt. If you know how many buttons, side by side, take up a given measurement, such as 5 buttons for every 8 cm (3¼ in), then you can work out how many you need overall. Always have a few extra buttons to hand.

2 Hand-sew a button on the hem of the skirt, making sure that the edge of the button abuts the hem and that the holes are straight.

3 Continue to sew buttons along the edge, making sure they are as close as possible, with no space between them, and that they are all aligned. Here the buttons have been sewn on to overlap each other.

Tip

For a more elaborate effect, combine buttons with different colours and shapes - small buttons interspersed with larger ones, square shapes with hearts. Novelty buttons in animal shapes would look sweet on children's sweaters, jackets or dresses.

Beaded Argyll

T HE UNEXPECTED COMBINATION of pretty pink beads with the Argyll pattern creates a modern classic. You can be a serious college girl without giving up one iota of girliness. Think New England in autumn with a shot of frivolity – and oh so much better than wearing pearls!

WHAT YOU NEED
- Grey Argyll wool sweater
- Ruler (optional)
- Chalk or pen fabric marker (optional)
- 1 container (about 400) pink glass beads
- Pink thread
- Scissors
- Sewing needle
- Tacking (basting) thread
- Beading needle

HOW TO DO IT

1 Place the sweater on a flat work surface, face up. Decide where you want the lines of beads on the front of the sweater. The easiest method is to follow the existing pattern, working the thin crisscrossing lines.

2 Alternatively, use the ruler and fabric marker to measure and mark out lines following the diagonal but halfway through the squares or parallel to the crisscrossing lines. Then sew a line of tacking (basting) stitches, regularly using a ruler to make sure that the lines are exactly straight. Before you start sewing, check the sweater visually from a distance.

3 Hand-sew the beads in place, following one diagonal line, or one tacked (basted) line, at a time. Sew each bead on separately, making two stitches through each one, and knot the thread securely on the wrong side. As you work, carefully abut each bead to the one before to make a continuous line, unbroken by spaces.

Beaded Heart Sweater

THE PERFECT SYMMETRY of the heart makes it an ideal motif for all kinds of decorative arts. This ancient symbol for love is worked onto the front and sleeves of a sweater for a romantic effect. Asymmetrical or elongated hearts are also good for creating a look that is more stylized.

WHAT YOU NEED

- Grey wool or cotton sweater
- Pen or chalk fabric marker
- Tape measure
- About 120 pale pink glass beads
- Grey thread
- Beading needle

Tip

Hearts are not the only shape that are simplistic in design yet potent in meaning. You could substitute stars, diamonds, a basic flower shape or even a sun or large asterisk combined with shorter, disconnected, beaded 'rays'.

HOW TO DO IT

1 Measure and mark a heart on the front centre of the sweater using the chalk or pen marker. To make sure it is centred, fold the sweater in half with the back sides together; the centre of the heart should fall on the centre fold line . It can be any size you like; here the heart measures 2.5 cm (1 in).

2 Thread the beading needle with the grey thread, knot it, and then bring it through from the reverse side of the sweater at the bottom tip of the heart. Thread on the first bead, re-enter the sweater along the marked line and repeat to make two stitches and knot on the underside. Continue sewing on the beads close together, following the marked line.

3 Repeat steps 1 and 2 to make hearts on the sleeves or, if desired, another on the back of the sweater.

Star-studded Corduroy

STUDS ARE NOT ONLY for denim and give extra punch to this deep pink corduroy skirt. Now that studs are available in star shapes, as well as in circles and colourful gemstones, the design possibilities are endless. For a bit of Hollywood glamour nearer to home, give your clothes a touch of stardom with this back pocket detailing.

WHAT YOU NEED
- Pink corduroy skirt with back pockets
- Tape measure
- Chalk or pen fabric marker
- 12 round studs and 2 star studs

HOW TO DO IT

1 Place the skirt on a flat work surface, with the pockets facing up. Measure and mark the positions for the star on each pocket by measuring halfway across the open top side of the pocket and measure slightly less than halfway down the length. Make a dot at these points with the chalk or pen marker.

2 Mark the positions for the round studs. Measure halfway down one side of the pocket and make a dot just inside the seam edge with the fabric marker. Repeat on the other side seam edge of the pocket. Make two more equally spaced marks for the other studs on each side of the star so that they make a slightly curved line up to the star in the middle.

3 Check that the marked dots are equally spaced and that the design is curved enough. Then repeat step 2 for the other pocket. Hold the skirt up to make sure that the marks on both pockets match.

4 Firmly press the star stud into the fabric at the marked position for the star. On the reverse side, bend back the prongs with your finger or a teaspoon to secure the stud in place. Continue the process to insert the round studs. Repeat for the other pocket.

Star-studded White Jeans

WHAT YOU NEED
- White jeans
- Tape measure
- 'Invisible' or 'fade away' pen fabric marker
- 20 metal star studs

HOW TO DO IT
Mark the position for the star-shaped studs along the back yoke of the jeans, making sure they are equally spaced. Insert one stud at a time, as described in step 4 above.

Glitzy Denim
Jacket

THINK RHINESTONE COWBOY and decorate
a plain denim jacket with sequin trims
and a confetti of coloured gemstones. This
version uses predominately turquoise and
pink, but you could try red and black for a
hard-edged look, or whatever combination
works with the colours in your wardrobe.

WHAT YOU NEED

- Denim jacket
- 1 pink leaf sequin appliqué
- Pins
- Pink and turquoise sewing
  thread
- Sewing needle
- Tape measure
- Scissors
- Double-width turquoise
  sequin trim
- Pink sequin trim
- Turquoise metallic cord
- Chalk or pen fabric marker
- 5 red and 5 pink gemstone
  star beads
- Clear 'invisible' thread
- Beading needle
- 60 round gemstone studs in
  assorted colours

HOW TO DO IT

1 Place the denim jacket, with the front facing up, on
a flat work surface. Position the sequin appliqué motif
on one collar lapel and pin it in place. Then use the pink
thread and a slipstitch to hand-sew around the edge
of the appliqué motif to secure it (see page 143).

2 Measure all the way around the edge of the collar
and cut a length of double turquoise sequin trim to size.
Starting at one corner, pin the trim in place around the
back of the collar, flush with the edge. When you reach
the other corner, cut off the surplus trim flush with the
edge. Then pin the trim along the two short lengths of
the collar, butting the ends together. Hand-sew the
sequin trim in place along both long sides using a
slipstitch and the turquoise thread.

3 Measure the horizontal seams above the pockets on
both sides of the jacket and cut lengths of pink sequin
trim to size, adding an extra 1 cm (½ in) to each one.
Working from the side seams in, pin the two lengths
in place, overlapping the trim onto the inside of the
central fastening. Hand-sew in place using the pink
thread and following the centre stitching in the trim.

4 Measure the edge of the pocket flap and cut two
lengths of turquoise metallic cord to size. Slipstitch a
length of cord to the edge of each pocket flap using the
turquoise thread. Secure each end with a few overcast
or couching stitches to prevent fraying (see page 143).

5 Hand-sew the red and pink star beads to the lapels
of the collar. Use the fabric marker to make dots on the
collar where you want the stars to be positioned. Sew
on each bead separately, making two stitches through
each one and knotting securely on the wrong side.

6 Add a sprinkling of coloured gemstones studs all
over the top panel of the jacket on both sides. If desired,
mark positions for the gemstones, as for the stars in
step 5; otherwise, just place them randomly. To insert
each gemstone, push the pronged piece through the
denim from the wrong side. Insert the gemstone into
the centre and bend the prongs around the stone.

Glitzy
Red Sequins

GO FROM DAY TO NIGHT by giving a sexy touch to a classic, demure polo neck (turtleneck) with sequin edging, showing there's more to be discovered behind your well-behaved ladylike exterior. An ideal top for when you need to present a refined elegance but don't want to look boring.

WHAT YOU NEED
- Red polo neck (turtleneck)
- Tape measure
- Narrow red sequin trim
- Scissors
- Pins
- Red elastic thread
- Sewing needle

TAKE A POLO NECK (TURTLENECK) SWEATER THAT YOU HAVE TIRED OF

HOW TO DO IT

1 Measure the cuffs and neck edge of the sweater and cut three lengths of sequin trim to size, adding 1 cm (½ in) extra to each one.

2 Pin the sequin trim to the right side of the fabric at the edges of the cuffs and the folded-over edge of the neck. Join the trim ends at the seams by overlapping.

3 Hand-sew the sequin trim in place, using the elastic thread. Make tiny running stitches, following the row of stitching through the centre of the trim.

Barely-There LBD

STRAPPY, BARELY-THERE LITTLE BLACK dresses never go out of fashion, but even they can look a little uninspiring and in need of a lift after you have worn them a zillion times. Hand-sew the sequin-covered ribbon in place so you can unpick it later if you wish and revert back to your tried-and-true original.

WHAT YOU NEED
- Black satin dress with spaghetti straps
- Scissors
- Tape measure
- 1 cm- (⅜ in-) wide red velvet ribbon
- Black thread
- Pins
- Sewing needle
- Black sequin ribbon trim

HOW TO DO IT

1 Remove the straps of the dress by unpicking the stitching or carefully cutting them away. Measure the straps and replace them with two lengths of red velvet ribbon cut to the same size. Pin and machine- or hand-stitch the ribbons in place on the wrong side.

2 Measure the whole way around the top edge of the dress. Cut a length of sequin trim to size, plus an extra 1 cm (½ in) for joining the ends. Pin the sequin trim around the top of the dress, joining the ends at a side seam by turning them under and abutting the short raw ends of the ribbon.

3 Hand-sew the sequin trim to the dress using tiny slipstitches along both long sides of the ribbon (see page 143).

THAT LITTLE BLACK DRESS THAT HAS PROVED SO USEFUL BUT NEEDS A LIFT

Tip
These dangling jewelled sequins will add instant eye-catching glamour when they are stitched along the cuffs and hem of a little black cardigan or crocheted top. Alternatively, sew them along the hem of a skirt or cropped black trousers for another fun and jazzy eveningwear idea.

Beaded Satin Trousers

A SPRINKLING OF CANDY-COLOURED beads looks good enough to eat. They add just enough decoration to give a pair of blue-grey tailored trousers some spanking new groove. The bright red, yellow, white and blue beads not only liven up the grey colour, but also provide textural relief to the satiny fabric.

WHAT YOU NEED

- Blue grey satin trousers
- 400 round and straight small glass beads, in assorted colours
- Blue-grey sewing thread
- Beading needle
- Scissors
- Tape measure

HOW TO DO IT

1 Starting at the hem of one trouser leg, sew on assorted coloured and shaped beads in a triangular formation using the beading needle and the blue-grey thread. Here the triangle measured 8 x 10 cm (3 ½ x 4 in), with the centre of the triangle on the seam. Sew each bead on with two stitches, knotting securely on the wrong side of the trousers.

2 Once you have sewn the beaded triangle shape, sew a line of beads up the side seam of the trouser leg. Here about 200 beads were used per leg.

3 Repeat steps 1 and 2 on the other trouser leg.

Diamanté Jeans

TRIM WITH TINY DIAMANTÉ studs decorate the side seams of bootleg jeans, giving rock-chick styling to a wardrobe basic. The eye-catching sparkly gems instantly elevate these jeans to hot party wear – just team them with a skimpy top and strappy heels for effortless glamour. Even better, the vertical line helps to visually lengthen the leg.

WHAT YOU NEED

- Jeans
- Tape measure
- Diamanté trim
- Scissors
- Pins
- Black sewing thread
- Sewing needle

Tip

Use the same approach for the side seams of black trousers or a pencil skirt. This type of delicate diamanté trim could also be sewn in parallel horizontal lines around a skirt or worked in diagonals across it.

HOW TO DO IT

1 Measure the side seam of the jeans and cut two lengths of diamanté trim to size, plus an extra 1 cm (½ in) on each length.

2 Starting just below the waistband, pin the trim along the side seams of the jeans, flush to the bottom of the waistband and turning the overlap under at the bottom hem.

3 Hand-sew the trim in place along both long edges using a slipstitch and the black thread (see page 143).

Leopard
skin-lined Skirt

EVERY GIRL NEEDS a hot little number for dates, parties and playtime. Vamp it up with sequins and super-sexy leopardskin that will look seductive whether you are perching on a barstool or sashaying through a dark nightclub. Wear this skirt with a matching camisole and vertiginous heels to bring out the animal in you.

WHAT YOU NEED
- Side-slashed straight black wool skirt
- Scissors
- Tape measure
- Leopard satin lining fabric, pre-washed and pressed
- Sewing machine
- Pins
- Iron and ironing board
- Black thread
- Black sequin trim
- Sewing needle

HOW TO DO IT

1 Remove the original lining from the skirt by unpicking the seams. To calculate how much leopardskin fabric you will need for the lining, first measure the length and then the width of each piece of original lining, including all the seam allowances and hems. Add up the total length and total width to get the final measurement. If in doubt, always purchase more fabric than you think you will need.

2 Use the pieces of original lining as a pattern to cut out the satin leopardskin fabric. Press the pieces flat, and then pin them right-sides down onto the wrong side of the leopardskin fabric, aligning them with the fabric grain. Cut out the pieces, allowing for any seam allowance or hem that you were unable to unpick.

Tip
Try lining a simple, chic black skirt with vibrant purple, hot pink or red satin for a more sophisticated, less vampish look. If you prefer, the lining can be hand-sewn along the side slits rather than left hanging, as shown here.

3 Turn under and press the seam allowance on all pieces. Machine-stitch the pieces together along the long side seams. Follow the original lining as a guide; for example, if the skirt has a zip, stitch only as far along the seam as the zip; if it has a side slit, stitch only to that point. Press the seams open on the stitched areas.

4 Before you attach the new lining, stitch the sequin trim to the skirt. Turn the skirt right-sides out. Measure the side seams from the waist to the slits and cut out two lengths of black sequin trim to size, adding 1 cm (½ in) to each. Pin a length of sequin trim along each side seam, ending where the slit begins, and turn under the raw ends. Hand-sew the trim in place, using a running stitch and following the line of stitching on the trim.

5 Turn the skirt wrong sides out and pin the lining to the skirt at the waistband seam, aligning it with the zip and side seams. At the zip, fold under the seam allowance on the lining and pin neatly to the zip tape. Hang the skirt up and check that the lining hangs straight, is smooth and doesn't pucker.

6 Slipstitch the lining to the skirt along the waistband and then to the zip tape, taking care not to sew through to the right side of the skirt.

7 At each slit, fold under the seam allowance twice and pin it in place (you will need to cut into the seam allowance at the top of the slit). At the bottom hem, turn under the seam allowance twice, mitre the corners at the slit sides and pin in place. Check and adjust the length of the hem if necessary. Hand-hem all the raw edges along the bottom edge and slits of the skirt to finish. The lining is free-hanging at the slits and hem.

Pink Sequin Camisole

DANCE THE NIGHT AWAY wearing this sequinned top and you'll out-sparkle the disco mirror ball. Nothing is sexier and slinkier than lingerie-style camisoles in vibrant eatable colours, like this luscious juicy pink. The shimmering sequinned detailing screams 'look at me'.

WHAT YOU NEED

- Pink cotton camisole
- Tape measure
- Scissors
- Pink sequin trim
- Pins
- Pink sewing thread
- Sewing needle

HOW TO DO IT

1 Measure the straps of the camisole and cut two lengths of pink sequin trim to size, adding an extra 1 cm (½ in) to each one.

2 Measure around the top edge of the camisole and cut a length of the same sequin trim to size, adding an extra 1 cm (½ in) to the measurement.

3 Pin the sequin trim to the straps, turning under each short end by 5 mm (¼ in). Hand-sew the trim in place, using pink thread and a running stitch and following the centre stitching line on the trim.

4 In the same way, pin and hand-sew the sequin trim round the neckline of the camisole. Join the ends at one side seam, turning under one short end and overlapping it on the other.

Turquoise Beaded Cardigan

B E A 1950S SWEATER GIRL in this pastel beaded cardigan, which is the perfect foil to the sharp lines of a pencil skirt or which can be teamed with flirty skirts and romantic chiffon dresses. Simply drape it over your shoulders and fasten a single button.

WHAT YOU NEED

- 80-100 straight turquoise glass beads, 3 cm (1¼ in) long
- Turquoise thread
- Beading needle
- Scissors
- Pink round-necked cardigan
- Pattern paper and pencil, or 1 m (39 in) of 115 cm- (45 in-) wide calico (muslin)
- Chalk or pen fabric marker
- 1 m (39 in) of 115 cm- (45 in-) wide turquoise satin lining, pre-washed and pressed
- Tape measure
- Pins
- Iron and ironing board
- Pink thread
- Sewing needle

HOW TO DO IT

1 Sew clusters of beads to the front of the cardigan. To do this, thread the beading needle with turquoise thread and knot the end. Make several small stitches through the front of the cardigan and knot them together on the reverse side. Then stitch through the cardigan and thread on 3-4 turquoise beads. Re-enter the same hole, come up again, and thread through one of the beads then back through the same hole, securing the cluster by knotting through the threads on the reverse side. Repeat the process to make 10-15 clusters on each side of the front of the cardigan.

2 Turn the cardigan wrong side out and place it on a flat work surface. Now you need to make three pattern template pieces for the lining: two for the sides and one for the back. The sleeves will not be lined.

3 Starting with one of the sides, pin the pattern paper or calico (muslin) to the inner side and use a pen or pen fabric marker to mark along the seams and about 2 cm (¾ in) from the bottom edge. Cut out the pattern and check that it follows the shape of the side piece of the cardigan and is flush with the front opening and neckline. The piece should be the exact size of the

finished lining for that section of the cardigan. Mark the top side. Repeat to make pattern pieces for the opposite side and the back.

4 Pin the three pattern pieces, top sides down, to the wrong side of the turquoise lining fabric, aligning them with the fabric grain. Using chalk or a pen fabric marker, mark around the template, adding 1 cm (½ in) seam allowance all round. Cut out each piece.

5 Turn under and press the seam allowance on all sides of each piece of the lining. Clip the armhole sections halfway through the seam allowance only, to help the fit smoothly around the curves.

6 Working on a side piece first, pin the lining right-side up to the inside of the cardigan, making sure the fabric fits smoothly. Using the pink thread, neatly slipstitch the lining in place along all the edges and making sure that the stitches only catch the wool so they do not appear on the right side (see page 143).

7 Repeat step 6 to attach the other side piece and then the back piece, abutting the pieces flush with each other where they join .

Indian
Goddess
T-shirt

TAKE ONE PLAIN WHITE T-SHIRT AND HEY PRESTO ...

A N INDIAN GODDESS image is decorated with a profusion of sequins and beads, creating a multicoloured one-of-a-kind effect. If you can't find a similar T-shirt, take an image you like to a colour-copy or T-shirt transfer printing shop and ask for it to be transfer-printed onto a white T-shirt. You could choose a picture of your own 'goddess' – Madonna or Britney, perhaps (a favourite rock-concert T-shirt can get a new lease of life this way).

WHAT YOU NEED
- White cotton T-shirt with 'goddess'-type design
- Cardboard
- 150 assorted sequins and 100 assorted beads
- Clear 'invisible' thread, or coloured threads
- Beading needle
- Scissors
- Ruler
- Chalk or pen fabric marker

HOW TO DO IT

1 Place the T-shirt on a flat work surface and slip a piece of card inside it to prevent you from stitching through to the other side.

2 Arrange beads and sequins on the design to high-light different areas. Hand-sew each one in place with a few stitches, knotting securely on the reverse of the T-shirt. For a more layered effect, sew smaller sequins on top of large ones or use sparkly beads to anchor the sequins (the bead will need to be bigger than the sequin hole). Bring the thread through the sequin, then thread on a bead and re-enter through the same hole in the sequin, knotting on the reverse side.

3 Using the fabric marker and a ruler, draw a faint square line 5 cm (2 in) from the edge of the printed image. Sew an assortment of different sequins in various colours, shapes and sizes along the line. Stitch an intersecting series of long straight beads, small round sequins and larger sequins to link the square outline 'frame' with the printed image.

Kaleidoscopic Dots

WHAT YOU NEED
- Black cotton round-neck top
- Piece of cardboard
- Chalk or pen fabric marker
- Ruler or tape measure
- Strong fabric glue
- 22-28 flat-backed gemstones in assorted colours
- Tweezers

DOTS ARE HOT and these are sparkly to boot. The brilliance of the gemstones against a dark colour makes a light-catching kaleidoscope. They can be used to add some groove to anything from a chic black top to a pair of bootleg jeans. Horizontal rows create a simple design, while diagonal rows on only one shoulder create an asymmetrical 1980s effect.

HOW TO DO IT

1 Place the top on a flat work surface and insert a piece of cardboard to separate the front from the back and to provide a firm surface on which to work.

2 Use a fabric marker to mark the points where you want to position the gemstones. Here there are four diagonal rows of increasing numbers of gemstones across the right shoulder of the top. To do this, start with the top row and marks dots for four equally spaced gemstones. Continue with the other rows, measuring to make sure the rows are equally spaced and using the row before as a guide for positioning the gemstones.

3 Dab small amounts of glue onto several of the marks at a time and stick on the gemstones using the tweezers. Alternate the colours so the same colours are not next to, or above or below, each other.

4 Once all the gemstones are attached, leave the top on the flat work surface overnight to dry.

Mosaic Gemstone Jeans

WHAT YOU NEED
- Denim jeans
- Chalk or pen fabric marker
- Tape measure
- Strong fabric glue
- 80 large oval, round and square flat-backed gemstones in assorted colours
- Tweezers

HOW TO DO IT

Working on the front of the jeans first, mark the positions for two rows of gemstones on the hem of both trouser legs. Make sure that the rows are straight and equally spaced from the hem. Work the bottom row first, positioning the gemstones as described in step 3, above, and varying the shapes. Glue on the second row and leave to dry before turning the jeans over and repeating on the back.

Flirty Frilled Skirt

THE CLASSIC SEAMSTRESS'S method of lengthening skirts is given a new slant with a chiffon ra-ra edge and sequin trim. This fun, flippy skirt, adapted from a red bias-cut version, presents a flirty romantic look, marrying heavier, sophisticated, velvet with springy, youthful, chiffon. The sequin trim can be in a colour to match the skirt, or in silver, gold or a contrasting colour.

WHAT YOU NEED

- Red velvet skirt
- Tape measure
- Chalk fabric marker
- Scissors
- Red chiffon
- Pins
- Sewing machine
- Red sewing thread
- Pink sequin trim

HOW TO DO IT

1 Place the skirt on a flat work surface and unpick the hem to reveal the raw edges. Measure around the circumference of the hem. Cut a length of chiffon on the bias to this measurement, adding an extra 3 cm (1¼ in). The chiffon frill can be any width you prefer, depending on the length you want the skirt to be; here the frill measures 15 cm (6 in) deep.

2 Fold the chiffon strip in half lengthways with right sides facing and pin the short raw edges together. Slide the band onto the hem of the skirt to check that the band fits, leaving a seam allowance of 1.5 cm (⅝ in) for the short ends to be joined.

3 Remove the chiffon band, adjust as necessary, and machine-stitch the short ends together with right sides facing to make a band. Overlock the raw edges of the seam allowance with a zigzag stitch.

4 Pin the chiffon band onto the bottom of the skirt with right sides together and long raw edges aligned. Make sure the joined ends of the chiffon band are at one of the skirt's side seams. Machine-stitch the chiffon to the skirt. Overlock the raw edges of the seam allowance with a zigzag stitch to prevent fraying.

5 Open out the chiffon band and press along the seam on the right side. Cut a length of sequin trim to measure the circumference of the skirt along the join of the chiffon. Pin in place to cover the stitched seam, joining the ends by turning under one short end and overlapping it onto the other at a side seam. Hand-sew the trim in place along both long edges using a slipstitch and the red thread (see page 143).

6 Finally turn under, press and pin a narrow double hem along the raw edge of the chiffon. Machine-stitch the hem in place or hand-sew using a slipstitch (see page 143).

Sweetheart T-shirt

A RIBBON-AND-BEAD TRIM in candy pink transforms a plain white T-shirt into the sweetest top, perfect for wearing with capris or lightweight skirts in summer. Do, however, choose a T-shirt that is form-fitting for the best results, perhaps with short sleeves, as here, or with ¾-length sleeves. A loose shirt, or one with ribbing or a wide band around the neck or sleeves, is too sporty-looking for such a delicate treatment as this.

WHAT YOU NEED
- White cotton v-neck T-shirt
- 1.5 cm- (⅝ in-) wide pink satin ribbon
- Tape measure
- Pins
- About 200 small pink glass bugle beads
- 1 love heart gemstone
- Pink thread
- Scissors
- Sewing needle
- Beading needle

1 Measure the distance round the neckline, and cut a length of pink satin ribbon to size, plus about 10 cm (4 in) extra for turning under the ends and fitting.

2 Turn under one short end of the ribbon and pin it to the deep 'v' at the neckline. Pin the ribbon along the edge of the neckline, easing it around all corners. At the end, trim the ribbon if necessary and turn under the short end, pinning it in place to abut the other end. There will be a slight gathering along the inner side of the ribbon as it is eased, but this is part of the effect.

3 Hand-sew the ribbon trim in place along both long sides using a slipstitch. Remove the pins.

4 Hand-sew the pink bugle beads onto the ribbon at different angles for a 'scattered' look. Nestle some into the folds of the ribbon. Sew two stitches through each bead and knot on the underside of the T-shirt.

5 Finish by sewing a heart diamanté in the centre of the 'v' neckline to conceal the join.

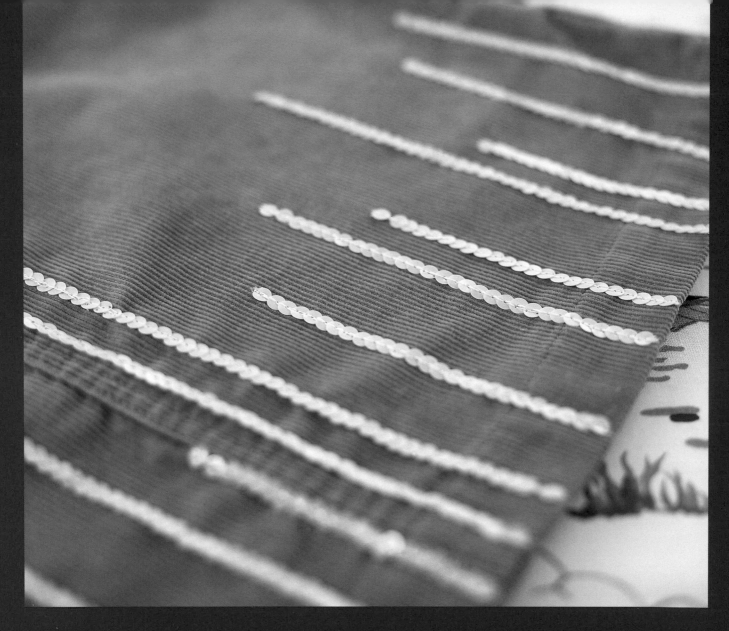

Rays of Light

A PALE BLUE CORDUROY SKIRT is 'dressed up' with rows of light-catching silver sequins, worked from the hem upward in strips of various lengths. Wear it cowboy-style with snakeskin boots and a denim jacket or go for a more feminine approach with blue fishnets and a sequinned top. Narrow-ribbed corduroy is more flattering than wide-whale.

WHAT YOU NEED

- 1.5 m (60 in) silver sequin trim
- Scissors
- Blue corduroy skirt
- Pins
- Silver thread
- Chalk or pen fabric marker and ruler (optional)
- Sewing machine
- Sewing needle (optional)

HOW TO DO IT

1 Cut the sequin trim into several different lengths, ranging from 12 cm (4 ¾ in) to 24 cm (9 ½ in). Place the skirt on a flat work surface and arrange the lengths in vertical rows from the hem. You can either make a pattern by alternating short, medium, and long lengths in different spacings, or just arrange them randomly until you like the design.

2 Pin the lengths of sequin trim in place on the skirt with the ends flush with the hem. The pattern of the corduroy will help you position the lengths straight. Alternatively, use a ruler and fabric marker to make vertical lines and then cut the sequin trim to match.

3 Machine-stitch each length of sequin trim in place with a running stitch, through the centre of the trim. Sew towards the hem so that you can hold the trim taut to keep it straight. Alternatively, use a zigzag stitch set to the width of the trim, or hand-sew the sequin trim in place using a running stitch.

How-to Techniques

STUDS AND GEMSTONES add fashionable style to jeans, jackets, handbags and t-shirts. The techniques for applying them are so easy and quick that you will have almost instant results. You can decorate a t-shirt with studs in just a few minutes' time and wear it immediately – no fuss, no waiting and no tricky materials to use. Flat-backed gemstones and diamantés in every colour under the sun can be added with just a dab of fabric glue.

INSERTING STUDS

1 Measure and mark positions for the metal studs using a chalk or pen fabric marker. The studs look best positioned along a hem or seam and equally spaced apart.

2 Firmly press the stud into the fabric from the right side, at the desired position.

3 Turn the fabric to the wrong side and bend the prongs inward, using your thumb and fingers, a metal teaspoon or a screwdriver, to secure the stud in place.

ATTACHING SEQUINS

1 Dab a small amount of strong fabric glue onto the spots where you want to position the flat-backed gemstones.

2 Pick up the gemstone using a pair of tweezers and position it on the glue. Allow to dry before moving the fabric.

3

Appliqué & Embroidery

Appliqué is simply the process of stitching or bonding one shape of fabric onto another. Fusible webbings make the technique fast, easy and super-effective. Appliqué motifs, whether representational or abstract, can be used as decoration on their own or as a starting point for further embellishment. Embroidery adds a rich texture to clothing that can look as sublime or overstated as you like.

Abstract Flower

BREAK UP A GEOMETRIC monochrome with a bright abstracted floral. A chequerboard pattern makes the perfect contrasting background for something curvy, feminine, vibrant and glittery. Black-and-white stripes, op-art gyroscopes, zigzags or chevrons would all be good alternatives. This is a top that delivers a powerful visual punch, so you need attitude to wear it – it is definitely not one for the wallflowers.

TAKE ONE BLACK-AND-WHITE SWEATER …

WHAT YOU NEED

- Fabric with a print of a large rose-coloured flower
- Paper-backed fusible webbing
- Iron and ironing board
- Embroidery scissors
- Black-and-white checked sweater
- Large green glass bead
- Green thread
- Embroidery scissors
- Small flat-backed gemstones or diamantés
- Fabric glue

HOW TO DO IT

1 Following the webbing manufacturer's instructions, iron the paper-backed webbing onto the wrong side of the patterned fabric.

2 Cut out the flower shape with the embroidery scissors, cutting around and into all the detail of leaves and flower petals.

3 Place the sweater on the ironing board and check the position for the flower. Here the rose has been positioned on the upper right-hand corner. Peel the paper backing from the flower, place in position, cover with a cloth and iron according to the webbing manufacturer's instructions. Allow to cool.

4 Hand-sew a glass bead in the centre of the flower with green thread. Place a dab of fabric glue on the back of one of the gemstones and stick to one of the petals. Repeat to stick gemstones all over the flower.

Bunch of Red Roses

FOR THIS DESIGN, you will need a flower-patterned fabric with huge full-blown blooms on it. Here, a rose-print headscarf was used, but if you can't find roses, look for poppies or any other large red flower. Search second-hand and thrift shops for suitable fabric, or look at roll-ends of upholstery fabric on sale. Pansies or violets will look striking on a purple top, but as they are usually printed smaller, you may need more of them. A 'virtual garden' of peonies will make an intensely lush design.

WHAT YOU NEED

- Flowered fabric with at least 5 large roses
- Paper-backed fusible webbing
- Iron and ironing board
- Embroidery scissors
- Red cotton ¾-length sleeve top
- Pins
- 5 green or black gemstone studs

HOW TO DO IT

1 Following the webbing manufacturer's instructions, iron a length of webbing to the wrong side of the patterned fabric.

2 Cut out the rose shapes with the embroidery scissors, cutting around and into all the detail of leaves and flower frills. Here five shapes were cut out. Peel the paper backing off each rose.

3 Place the red cotton top on an ironing board and arrange the roses on the front. When you are happy with the positioning of the pieces, pin them in place. Iron each one by covering with a cloth and pressing the iron on top, according to the webbing manufacturer's instructions. Allow the top to cool.

4 Insert a gemstone stud into the centre of each rose. To do this, push the pronged piece through the fabric from the wrong side. Insert the gemstone into the centre and bend the prongs around the stone with your fingers or a metal teaspoon to secure it.

Zebraskin 'N' Flowers

ADD FLAIR TO A CASUAL TOP with zebra stripes, dotted with appliqué flowers. The curvy shapes of floral blooms help break up the harder lines of black and white. Using an initial stops the design from being too girly. Suede tape is available in a range of finishes and patterns, so use your imagination to combine it with your existing clothes and accessories. Try using it to create jazzy borders on bags, or to trim cuffs. The flowers can be purchased as ready-made appliqués, or cut out from a decorative ribbon or fabric remnant.

WHAT YOU NEED

· Iron-on zebra suede tape, measuring 3 cm (1¼ in) wide
· Lime-green sleeveless cotton top
· Scissors
· Pins
· Tape measure or ruler
· Iron and ironing board
· Ready-made embroidered rose appliqués
· Fabric glue

HOW TO DO IT

1 Cut out strips of the iron-on fabric tape to make the letter of your choice. Any letter with straight lines is suitable – such as A, E, F, H, K, L, M, N, T, V, W, X, Y or Z. Here 35 cm (13¾ in) of tape was used to make a 12-cm (4¾-in) high letter N.

2 Place the lime-green top flat on an ironing board and arrange the zebraskin tape pieces to form the letter. Pin the pieces in place, measuring to check that the letter is straight and centred.

3 Following the manufacturer's instructions, cover the tape with a cloth and iron in place, removing the pins in each section as you work. Allow to cool.

4 Position the four embroidered roses on the letter. Here they have been placed at each corner of the letter. When you are happy with their position, glue each one in place with fabric glue. Allow to dry.

Glitter Heart and Wings

COOL CLUBWEAR TO DANCE the night away – team this angel-heart top is some skinny hip-huggers and a pair of sexy strappy shoes for that oh so rock chick look. Combine velvet appliqué pieces with leopardskin or suede, then accent with glitter or sequins.

HOW TO DO IT

1 To make a template for the design, draw a heart free-hand onto the cardboard, then draw two wings – a right one and a left one – and cut out the three templates.

2 Place a piece of the fusible webbing on a work surface and lay the scrap of pink satin for the heart on top, right-side up. Pin together. Place the template on top, trace around it with the fabric marker, and then cut out the heart shape through both layers. Repeat the process to cut out the two wings from the leopardskin fabric and webbing. Treat each shape as one piece.

3 Alternatively, if you are using paper-backed fusible webbing, you can iron-fuse the webbing to the wrong side of the fabric, draw the shapes directly onto the paper side, cut out and then peel off the paper before fusing it in place (see Bunch of Red Roses, pages 60–1).

4 Place the top on the ironing board and centre the heart on the front, making sure that the fusible webbing is exactly aligned underneath and the design is centred. Following the webbing manufacturer's instructions, carefully place a cloth over the heart and hold a hot iron on top until the cloth is dry. Do not slide the iron back and forth. Lift the cloth off. Repeat to iron on the wings, abutting them neatly to the sides of the heart.

5 Machine-stitch around the heart and wing shapes, using a close zigzig stitch. Use pink thread for the heart and black thread for the wings.

6 Place the top on a flat work surface. Cover the heart with a generous amount of fabric glue, using the brush to spread it evenly. Sprinkle on the machine-washable sequins. Leave to dry overnight. To finish, shake the top onto newspaper to remove any loose sequins.

WHAT YOU NEED
- Cardboard and pen
- Scissors
- Chalk or pen fabric marker
- Fusible webbing
- Pins
- Scrap of bright pink satin for the heart
- Scraps of leopardprint satin
- Red cotton spaghetti-strap top
- Pink and black thread
- Fabric glue for sequins and glitter
- Paintbrush
- Machine-washable pink heart sequins
- Iron and ironing board
- Sewing machine
- Scissors

THE POPULAR FASHION for adding decoration to the hems of jeans takes a twist here with leather and tweed. Cut-outs in buttery cream and chocolate brown leather complement the tailored look of tan tartan trousers, giving pretty detailing to a classic style. If you can't afford Bottega Veneta, or cleverly cut Joseph leather trousers, inexpensive leather scraps can be cut out in any shape and size you like and patched-and-pieced to thick felt handbags, tweedy skirts or even Burberry-style checked scarves.

Leather-detailed Checked Trousers

WHAT YOU NEED

- Cardboard and pen
- Scissors
- Scraps of leather in cream and chocolate
- Brown tartan-checked trousers
- Pins
- Ochre and brown stranded cotton embroidery thread
- Embroidery needle
- Tape measure
- Beading needle
- Clear 'invisible' thread
- 12-14 yellow or clear beads
- 30-40 small flat-backed gemstones
- Strong fabric glue

HOW TO DO IT

1 Make two cardboard templates for the flowers by drawing a large and a small flower shape freehand onto the cardboard and cutting them out. Here the cream flowers measure 8 x 10 cm (3¼ x 4 in) and the chocolate flowers are 5 x 8 cm (2 x 3¼ in).

2 Trace around the large template onto the back of the cream leather and then trace round the small one onto the back of the chocolate-brown leather. Cut out and repeat to make two flowers in each colour and size.

3 Place the trousers on a flat work surface and position one cream and one chocolate flower cut-out onto the end of each trouser leg, measuring to match the positioning on both legs. When you are happy with the positions of the cut-outs, pin them in place.

4 Insert a piece of card inside one leg to prevent stitching through to the other side. Using one strand of embroidery thread, tack (baste) the leather flowers in place with short stab stitches (see page 143). Repeat on the other trouser leg to secure the leather cut-outs.

5 Using the beading needle, attach several beads to the centre of each flower. Secure each bead with two stitches through the leather and fabric.

6 Using one strand of embroidery thread in ochre and brown, embroider around each flower with assorted stitches. If desired, insert a piece of cardboard between the trouser legs to make stitching easier. Here a stem stitch was combined with large daisy (detached chain) stitches to make the stems and leaf shapes. You may also like to try other embroidery stitches, such as feather or fern stitches (see page 143).

7 To finish, glue a scattering of small coloured and clear gemstones around the flowers and onto the trouser fabric with strong fabric glue. Apply a dab of fabric glue to the reverse side of each gemstone and stick in place. Work one trouser leg at a time, allowing the first to dry before repeating on the other leg.

Pink Poodle

UPDATE THE 1950s CLASSIC American poodle skirt with an appliquéd and embroidered poodle pet on a bubble-gum pink sweater. It is a little nod to the days of bobby socks, ponytails, fluffy sweaters, full skirts and saddle shoes. Or think of it as an LA moment and make your appliqué a carbon copy of your own real dog; talking your dog for a walk while wearing the sweater could be just so California kitsch. Another variation is to make a giant dog face from brown felt, transfer it to the centre front of a sweatshirt and decorate with studs for the collar, embroidered details and glittery diamanté eyes.

WHAT YOU NEED

- Pale pink brush cotton fabric
- Paper-backed fusible webbing
- Iron and ironing board
- Scissors
- Pen
- Hot pink sweater
- Pink, gold and turquoise thread
- Scissors
- Needles: sewing, embroidery and beading
- Sewing machine
- Pins
- Gold ribbon
- Red and black stranded cotton embroidery thread
- Turquoise ribbon

HOW TO DO IT

1 Following the webbing manufacturer's instructions, iron the paper-backed fusible webbing to the wrong side of the pink cotton fabric.

2 Draw the outline of a poodle onto the backing paper and cut it out. If you are unsure about drawing freehand, copy or trace the outline of a poodle from a picture or stencil. Remember that the poodle will be facing the opposite way to how you draw it. Here the poodle measures 9 x 10 cm (3½ x 4 in).

3 Place the sweater on the ironing board, making sure it is flat. Arrange the poodle on the sweater until you are happy with its position. Here it has been placed on the bottom right-hand corner.

4 Remove the backing paper and iron the poodle in position by covering it with a cloth and pressing the iron on top, according to the manufacturer's instructions. Make sure you do not slide the iron back and forth over the design.

5 Stitch a decorative machine-stitch or hand-sew a blanket stitch (see page 143) around the poodle with the pink thread. For the lead (leash), pin the gold ribbon in place, from the neck of the poodle in a curved loop. Machine-stitch to secure, using a close zigzag stitch and gold thread, and turning under the short end.

6 Hand-embroider the features using a single strand of embroidery thread. Use a French knot in black for the eye (see page 143). Use a backstitch in red for the mouth and satin stitch in black for the feet (see page 143).

7 To make the collar, pin and hand-stitch turquoise ribbon along the neck, turning under the short ends. Sew three pink beads equally spaced out on the collar using the beading needle, and making two stitches to secure each bead. Sew 1 large multifaceted glass bead to cover the join between the collar and the lead (leash).

Rose Denim Skirt

APPLIQUÉD ROSES TRANSFORM a denim skirt into a work of art. Redouté-inspired splashes of full-blown blossoms are worked into a tiered design, reminiscent of a trelliswork of old-fashioned garden roses. The deep red colour stands out in sharp contrast from the dark denim background, but you can vary the effect depending on the fabric you have at hand. Pale pink flowers, for example, would work well against either a pale blue distressed denim or a pink skirt.

WHAT YOU NEED

- Floral furnishing fabric
- Paper-backed fusible webbing
- Iron and ironing board
- Embroidery scissors
- Dark denim skirt
- Red and dark red fabric paints
- Small paintbrush
- 100 red and green glass beads in various shapes
- Red and green thread
- Beading needle

HOW TO DO IT

1 Following the webbing manufacturer's instructions, iron a length of paper-backed fusible webbing to the wrong side of the patterned fabric.

2 Cut out the flower and leaf shapes with the embroidery scissors, cutting around and into all the detail of leaves and flower frills. Peel the paper backing off each shape.

3 Place the denim skirt on an ironing board and arrange the roses on the front. Iron each one in place by covering with a cloth and pressing the iron on top, according to the instructions. Work one piece at a time. Allow the skirt to cool.

4 Add extra colour to the roses with the fabric paint and a brush. Use red to intensify the colour of the roses, and highlight details in the darker red. Leave the skirt to dry overnight on a flat work surface.

5 When dry, embellish the leaves, roses and surrounding area with beadwork. Sew each bead on separately, making two stitches through each one, and knot securely on the wrong side of the skirt.

Embroidered Felt Flowers

ON HIGH-NECKED TOPS, where necklaces are difficult to wear, an embroidery-and-felt design is an accessory of its own. Knitwear, such as this lilac sweater, makes an ideal background for homespun decoration.

WHAT YOU NEED

- Cardboard and pen
- Scissors
- Pink and mauve felt
- Lilac polo neck (turtleneck)
- Strong fabric glue
- Paintbrush
- Pink, pale pink, red stranded cotton embroidery thread
- Embroidery needle
- Gold, pink and red glass beads and sequins
- Clear or coloured thread
- Beading needle

HOW TO DO IT

1 Make a cardboard template for the flower by drawing a flower shape onto the cardboard and cutting it out. Here the flower measures 3 x 3 cm (1¼ x 1¼ in).

2 Trace round the flower shape onto the felt and cut out to make one mauve and two pink flowers.

3 Place the sweater on a flat work surface. Decide on the positioning of the flowers by arranging them on the sweater. Apply a small dab of fabric glue on the reverse of each flower with a paintbrush and secure them in place. Allow to dry.

4 Use one strand of embroidery thread to stitch stab stitches into the centre of each flower, radiating outward (see page 143). If desired, insert a piece of card between the layers of the sweater to aid stitching.

5 Using the beading needle and clear or coloured thread, sew small glass beads at the ends of each stab stitch, making two stitches through each bead.

6 Anchor one sequin to the centre of each flower using a bead. To do this, bring the thread through the sequin, thread on a bead, and re-enter through the same hole in the sequin, knotting the thread on the reverse side.

7 Using one strand of embroidery thread, embroider tendrils around and connecting the flower shapes using chain, feather or stem stitches (see page 143).

Black Outline
Flower

THE STRIKING BLACK-ON-TURQUOISE colours enhance the pictorial quality of this flower design. Here the image was taken as an enlarged photocopy of a line drawing from a (copyright-free) flower book, but look through magazines and books for inspiration and then draw your own freehand design. For a more Op-Art effect, stitch overlapping concentric circles, squiggles or spirals.

WHAT YOU NEED
- Cardboard or paper and a pen
- Scissors
- Turquoise sleeveless top
- Pins (for a paper template)
- 'Invisible' or 'fade away' pen fabric marker
- Thick black sewing thread
- Sewing needle

HOW TO DO IT
1 Make a template by drawing a flower shape onto paper or cardboard and cutting it out. Here a 10 x 10 cm (4 x 4 in) flower shape was used.

2 Place the top on a flat work surface and arrange the template in position on a bottom corner of the top. When you are happy with the placement, trace round the template onto the top using the pen fabric marker. If you are using a paper template, pin it in place before tracing. Remove the template and sketch in any extra detail on the flower freehand.

3 Place a piece of cardboard inside the top to keep the layers separate. Using thick black sewing thread and a needle, stitch over the flower outline using an even running stitch. Stitch the details within the flower.

4 To build up the design, highlight specific areas with extra stitching. Repeat a few rows of running stitch along various sections, such as on the inside of petal curves and the tips of the petals.

Vintage Lace with a **Lemon** Twist

Get the LA vibe with this neon mix of scorching yellow under brightest turquoise. Take joy in the unexpected: other hot colour combos that also work well are pink and turquoise, orange and yellow, or lime and cranberry. Think Day-Glo cocktails under palm trees by the beach, sweltering heat and an upfront, sassy attitude.

WHAT YOU NEED

- Old remnants of cotton lace and lace trim
- Embroidery scissors
- Turquoise fabric hand-dye
- Salt
- Yellow sleeveless cotton v-neck top
- Turquoise cotton thread
- Pins
- Cardboard
- Sewing needle

HOW TO DO IT

1 Make sure the lace is clean, dry and free of stains. Any damaged or marked areas can be simply cut away.

2 Following the dye manufacturer's instructions, dye the lace by hand in a plastic tub or basin. (Using a machine-dye and a washing machine may damage and unravel the lace.) You will need to use a quantity of salt, depending on the weight of the lace. After the specified time, rinse the lace pieces well and air-dry them.

3 When the lace is dry, place the top on a flat work surface and arrange the pieces on the front. Here a wide band of lace trim runs diagonally across the top, with another band running along the opposite top corner to complete the v-neck. An open laceworked piece has been combined with tighter-worked lace. A narrower band of trim completes the bottom border. A lace rose was placed on the point of the 'v'. When you are happy with the result, pin the pieces in place.

4 Insert card between the layers of the top and then, using the turquoise thread, hand-sew each piece in position using tiny, even stitches to secure. To clean the top, wash carefully in cold water, rinsing constantly, so the dye does not run. Do not soak.

Pink Heart
Skirt

OVERSIZED ISOLATED MOTIFS make an impact. This valentine-inspired heart is a stand-out-and-shout design that also gives a touch of romance to a ruffled red skirt. You can wear it girly and glamour-puss with fishnets and ankle boots or dress it down with trainers (sneakers) and a T-shirt. Choose any vibrant red and pink combo – try strawberry on Schiaparelli pink, vermillion on brick-red or layer the palest pastel pink on dusty rose.

WHAT YOU NEED

- Pink satin fabric
- Paper-backed fusible webbing
- Iron and ironing board
- Pen
- Scissors
- Red cotton skirt
- Sewing machine
- Pins
- Tape measure
- Pink thread

HOW TO DO IT

1 Following the webbing manufacturer's instructions, iron a length of webbing to the wrong side of the satin.

2 Draw the heart onto the backing paper, either by tracing round a cardboard or paper template, or by folding the fabric in half and drawing half a heart along the fold line. Here a 30 cm (11¾in) heart was used for a 50 cm- (20 in-) long red cotton skirt. Cut out the heart shape and peel off the backing paper.

3 Place the red skirt on an ironing board and arrange the heart on the centre front, measuring to ensure it is centred and straight. When you are happy with the positioning, pin the heart in place.

4 Because the heart is large, you will need to work one section at a time, from top to bottom. Remove the pins for one section, cover with a cloth and press the iron on top, according to the webbing manufacturer's instructions. Repeat as necessary to fuse the whole heart in place. Allow the skirt to cool.

5 Using the pink thread, machine-stitch around the edge of the heart using a close zigzag stitch.

An Initial 'P'

TAKING INSPIRATION from sports letters, this single letter will mark you out as an individual rather than a team member. The corduroy gives a rugged, sporty feel to the top, and the bright letter against a dark background will make you stand out from the crowd.

WHAT YOU NEED

· Yellow corduroy fabric
· Fusible webbing
· Iron and ironing board
· Cardboard or paper and pen
· Scissors
· Teal-blue sweatshirt
· Sewing machine
· Tape measure
· Yellow thread

Tip

Corduroy is available in a huge range of colours, but felt or denim would give an equally rugged-looking effect. Choose fabrics that are sympathetic to your top – don't try using corduroy on lightweight cotton, for example, and avoid slippery fabrics and those that fray easily.

HOW TO DO IT

1 Following the webbing manufacturer's instructions, iron the webbing to the wrong side of the corduroy.

2 Make a template by drawing a letter freehand onto cardboard, or printing out a copy of a letter in a large point size from your computer. Cut out the template.

3 Place the template the wrong way round (mirror writing) on the wrong side of the corduroy. Trace around it onto the backing paper of the webbing, and then cut out the letter.

4 Peel off the backing paper and place the letter on the centre front of the shirt. Measure to ensure that the letter is perfectly straight and centred.

5 Cover with a cloth, and press the iron on top, following the webbing manufacturer's instructions.

6 To finish, machine stitch around the edge of the letter with yellow thread, using a close zigzag stitch.

Buttoned-up Heart

EASIER AND LESS TIME-CONSUMING to sew on than sequins and beads are buttons. What's more, the choices are limitless: bone, shell, mother-of-pearl, brass, metal and wood are all are available in a medley of colours and shapes. Use this design as a starting point: you may like to continue a line of buttons along the hem of the T-shirt, or combine large buttons with tiny ones. Smaller felt hearts in different sizes could be sewn all over, with complementary buttons on each one – some as outlines, others in the centre. Or use another shape altogether – iconographic crosses in different styles and sizes can be appliquéd on, each encrusted with embroidery, buttons and beadwork.

WHAT YOU NEED

- Light grey craft felt
- Fabric marker pen
- Cardboard
- Scissors
- Dark grey cotton T-shirt
- Tape measure
- Fabric glue (or fusible webbing)
- Paintbrush
- 20 round pink buttons
- Grey thread
- Sewing needle

HOW TO DO IT

1 Using a fabric marker, draw a heart shape on the felt, either by tracing round a cardboard template, or by folding the felt in half and drawing half a heart along the fold line. Here the heart measures 8 cm (3 ¼ in) at its widest and 9 cm (3 ½ in) in height. Cut out the shape.

2 Place the T-shirt on a flat work surface and position the heart on the front centre. Measure to check that the design is centred and straight. Check that the buttons will work around the edge so that they abut each other. If there are too few buttons to go around, trim the heart to make it smaller and check again. Mark a guideline position for the heart with the fabric marker.

3 Use a paintbrush to spread the fabric glue evenly on one side of the heart and then press the heart in place. Alternatively, use fusible webbing (see Bunch of Red Roses, page 60) to attach the heart.

4 Thread the needle with grey thread and sew the buttons around the heart to cover the edge. The buttons should be placed as closely together as possible, with no gaps between.

Stepping Out

Mad about your Manolos? Passionate about footwear? These charming little motifs can be ironed on anywhere. Position one near the neckline, on a sleeve, pocket, or the back of the neck to look like a new trendy designer label or mix up a bunch of different shoe designs and iron on all over a cotton shoulder bag or the back of a jean jacket. If shoes don't excite you, there are lots of other ready-made motifs available, from floral and animal designs to more abstract shapes.

WHAT YOU NEED

- Long-sleeved black cotton T-shirt
- Iron-on embroidered shoe motifs
- Iron and ironing board
- Pins

HOW TO DO IT

1 Lay the T-shirt flat on an ironing board and arrange the shoe motifs as desired, then pin them in place. Here one motif was placed 10 cm (4 in) from the neckline.

2 For the first one, remove the pin, cover with a cloth, and iron in place to fuse, following the manufacturer's instructions. Repeat this for the remaining motifs, and allow to cool.

Butterfly Patch Jacket

TAKE ONE DENIM JACKET AND METAMORPHOSE ...

THINK WOODSTOCK with this retro hippie-style jean jacket. Adapt the glitter paint for the motif you have; you could try groovy 1960s and 1970s designs, such as a yellow smiley face, a mushroom (as sported on Kate Hudson's jeans), an ankh symbol or peace sign, or use a combination of different patches for an all-over acid-trip effect. If you like the butterfly motif, consider working repeats of the same iron-on all over the jacket, or source a really huge motif and work it on the back of the jacket, adding layers of different coloured glitter paint for an in-your-face design.

WHAT YOU NEED

- Jean jacket
- Blue iron-on butterfly
- Iron and ironing board
- Small paintbrush
- Turquoise and blue glitter paint
- Strong fabric glue
- 2 black flat-backed gemstones

HOW TO DO IT

1 Iron the embroidered butterfly motif on the top right-hand corner of the jacket by covering with a cloth and pressing the iron on top, according to the manufacturer's instructions. Leave to cool.

2 Paint glitter paint around the edge of the butterfly, and along the centre 'body' if desired, to give the motif a bit of sparkle. Leave to dry on a flat work surface.

3 Using the fabric glue, stick a black gemstone onto the end of each antennae.

How-to Techniques

S EQUINS ARE AVAILABLE in a huge variety of shapes and colours, such as hologram dots, hearts, multicoloured discs and stars. They can be used in the same way as machine-washable glitter – to fill in a design area with sparkling colour and texture, or they can be glued on individually. Choose flat machine-washable sequins without holes for this technique, and make sure you use a generous amount of strong glue.

SEQUIN HEARTS

1 Cut out a paper or cardboard heart template, Trace round the template onto the garment using an 'invisible' fabric marker.

2 Paint a generous amount of glue inside the heart. Use a glue that is compatible with the sequins and the same brand.

3 While the glue is still wet, liberally sprinkle the glittery heart sequins onto the glue, making sure no area of glue is visible.

4 Press lightly down on the sequins to ensure they stick. Leave to dry until the glue has hardened, preferably overnight.

5 When dry, shake off the excess sequins onto a piece of paper to reveal the design. The sequins can be reused.

How-to Techniques

If YOU ARE USING a plain or all-over patterned fabric, iron the fusible webbing to the entire length of the fabric; this way, you can cut out various shapes as you require them, without having to fuse more webbing onto scraps of fabric later on. The shapes you choose to draw or trace onto the paper can be as ornate or simple as you like, but remember you will need to machine-stitch around the edge of each appliquéd piece to prevent fraying.

WEB FUSING THE HEART

1 Refer to the manufacturer's instructions before you begin. Iron a length of fusible webbing onto the wrong side of the patterned fabric.

2 Cut out a paper or cardboard heart template and draw around it onto the protective paper of the webbing with a pen. Alternatively, draw a freehand image directly onto the backing paper.

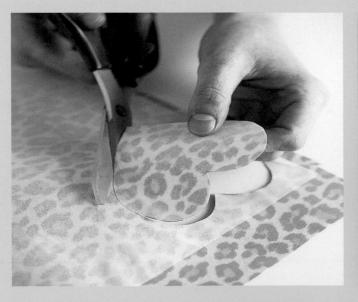

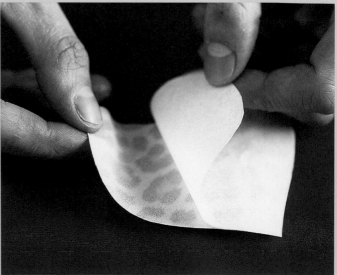

3 Cut out the heart shape from the fabric with a pair of sewing scissors, following the pen outline.

4 Peel off the protective backing paper. The appliqué is now ready to be positioned and fused in place on a garment.

How-to Techniques

CHINTZY FURNISHING FABRICS AND old-fashioned prints may not look stylish or even attractive as a whole, but they can offer up some great isolated designs to use for appliqué. Search your local charity or thrift shops for fabric remnants, old clothes and curtains that have an interesting design element. The motif doesn't have to be floral; you might find yourself inspired by a boy's cowboy pyjamas, a bird or wildlife print or a simple geometric.

WEB FUSING THE FLOWER

1 Refer to the manufacturer's instructions before you begin. Select the area of flower detail that you want to use and iron the fusible webbing onto the reverse of the fabric.

2 Cut out the flower from the fabric using a pair of sewing scissors. If desired, use embroidery scissors for cutting out shapes that have intricate, fine details or an irregular outline.

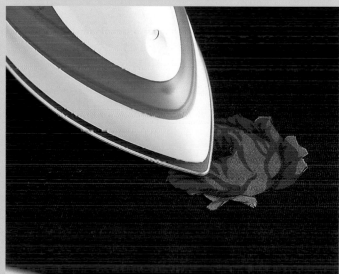

3 Peel off the protective backing paper from the fabric flower motif.

4 Position the appliqué on the garment. Following the manufacturer's instructions, fuse in place with a hot iron. Some manufacturers may recommend covering the appliqué motif with a cloth.

4

Printing & Painting

Exciting new products, from washable glitters and foils to puffa paints and stamp inks, make printing and painting on fabric both fun and inventive. Transfer prints enable a photograph to be copied onto T-shirts, and you can buy screen-printing equipment for creating your own designs. Whether you prefer stencilling or freehand design, the projects here will give you the opportunity to experiment.

Blue Star

THIS STAR AND GEMSTONE TOP invokes the spirited casual dressing of today's teen pop stars – all you need is bleached jeans, a diamanté belt and some killer boots to mimic their laid-back street-savvy style. You can either buy a star stencil from a home-decorating shop, or draw and cut one yourself.

HOW TO DO IT

1 Cover a flat work surface with newspaper. Place the vest (tank) top on the work surface and insert a piece of cardboard measuring the width and height of the top between the back and front layers.

2 If you are cutting your own stencil, draw a star onto the stencil card. Alternatively, trace a star from a book or magazine onto tracing paper with pencil, tape the tracing paper, lead side down, onto the stencil card and re-trace over it to transfer the image. Place the stencil card on a cutting mat and cut out the stencil with a craft knife (see page 107).

3 Position the stencil on the centre front of the shirt, about 10 cm (4 in) from the neckline. Measure to ensure it is centred and straight, then secure it in place with masking tape.

4 Dab the stencil brush into blue fabric paint and apply the paint to the top through the cut-out star (see page 107). Do not overload the brush or the paint will seep underneath the stencil. Reapply the paint, as necessary. When you are finished, remove the tape and carefully lift off the stencil. Wash the stencil brush immediately.

5 Along the neckline and between the shoulder straps, use a fabric marker to mark the points where you want to position the diamanté. Dab a small amount of fabric glue onto one mark at a time and stick on the gemstones using the tweezers.

6 Leave the top on the flat work surface for a few hours until the glue has hardened and the paint has dried. Follow the fabric paint manufacturer's instructions to fix the paint, usually by ironing onto the wrong side of the design.

WHAT YOU NEED

- Newspapers
- Grey cotton vest (tank top)
- Cardboard
- Stencil card, tracing paper, pencil or pen, cutting mat and craft knife, or a pre-cut star stencil
- Tape measure or ruler
- Masking tape
- Stencil brush
- Blue fabric paint
- Chalk or pen fabric marker
- Strong fabric glue
- 11 small silver flat-backed diamantés
- Tweezers
- Iron and ironing board

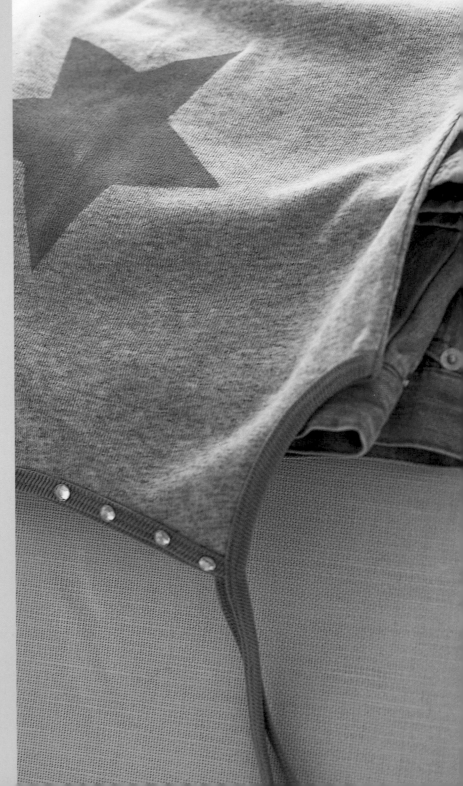

The Way of the East

ALTHOUGH THERE ARE A PLETHORA of printed tops for sale, if you have a favourite image you want on a T-shirt, you can easily make your own. Asian figures and motifs give an Eastern inspired edge to clothing, inviting romantic images of far-off destinations. Whether you are interested in yoga, Buddhism or the *I Ching*, or just like the stylized images of Eastern art, source an image that you respond to. Try Buddha, Siva or just a quaint little Chinese figure like the one here emblazoned across your chest.

WHAT YOU NEED

- Colour photocopy of a copyright-free Chinese character
- Scissors
- White long-sleeve T-shirt
- Tape measure or ruler

HOW TO DO IT

1 Take a colour photocopy of the Chinese character to a copy shop or T-shirt printing shop that offers colour transfers onto T-shirts. Ask the shop to photocopy the design onto transfer paper.

2 Cut out the design and take it back to the copier or printing shop with the long-sleeve white T-shirt. Centre the image on the front of the T-shirt, measuring to ensure that it is straight and centred. Ask the copier or shop to print the design as positioned.

Tip
You could also use the technique to create horizontal and vertical stripes in various widths, or cut out notches along the length of newspaper to make irregular shapes or sawtoothed lines.

HOW TO DO IT

1 Cover a flat work surface with newspaper or an old sheet, securing it with masking tape. Place the top, front side up, on the surface. Insert a piece of cardboard inside the top to separate the back and front layers.

2 Arrange pieces of plain newsprint on the top to create lines of varying widths for the first colour; here, three lines were created for the turquoise ink. Make sure the top is exposed only in the areas you want coloured – the rest of the top should be covered up with plain newsprint.

3 Place the screen over the top, taking care not to move the paper. Following the manufacturer's instructions, pour the first colour of ink (here, turquoise) in a line along the top end of the screen.

4 Using the squeegee or a piece of cardboard, and holding the screen down firmly with one hand, scrape the ink from end to end to print the lines onto the top, using an even, firm action. Dab the squeegee or cardboard to remove excess ink, and repeat to print over the top twice (see page 106). Carefully remove the screen and the paper. Discard the newspaper and immediately wash the screen and squeegee. Allow the ink to dry for the recommended time .

5 When dry, repeat steps 2 to 4 to make the yellow line, allowing the line to overlap onto the blue. Use fresh newspaper, the cleaned screen, and either the cleaned squeegee or a new piece of cardboard for each colour. Repeat the technique to make the pink line. You can make as many lines in as many colours as you like.

6 Wash the screen and the squeegee, and leave the top flat to dry for the recommended time. When dry, fix the printed design, if necessary, according to the screen-printing instructions.

Line by Line

A PLAIN WHITE T-SHIRT is printed with an abstract pattern of cut-out lines in a neon palette of colours inspired by modern art. Let screen-printing bring out the art student in you and research Pop and Abstract art movements for inspired designs.

WHAT YOU NEED

- Newspapers or an old sheet or fabric remnant
- Masking tape
- White vest (tank) top
- Cardboard
- Plain newsprint
- Scissors
- Screen-printing screen
- Turquoise, yellow and pink screen-printing inks
- Squeegee or long piece of cardboard

Stamp-printed Flowers

STAMP-PRINTING IS ONE OF THE EASIEST, and one of the earliest, methods for decorating textiles. Here a floral repeat motif is stamped onto a bright lime fluoro top, creating images that are uniform and possess an intricacy of design. The ink shades in areas and outlines, leaving other areas for the background to show through. Stamps in a variety of forms can be purchased from home-decorating shops or department stores.

WHAT YOU NEED
- Lime cotton vest (tank) top
- Cardboard
- 'Invisible' or 'fade away' pen fabric marker (optional)
- Tape measure or ruler
- Fabric stamping ink or paint
- Roller
- Rubber flower stamp
- Plain paper
- Iron and ironing board

HOW TO DO IT

1 Place the top on a flat work surface and insert a piece of cardboard, measuring the width and height of the top, between the front and back layers.

2 Here six flowers were stamped on randomly. If you prefer to work out placement first, measure and mark the central positions for the flowers with a small dot, using the fabric marker.

3 Roll the roller in the fabric stamping ink or paint and then roll the paint onto the surface of the rubber stamp.

4 Press the stamp onto the T-shirt and hold it down firmly so that all the details of the stamp print on the fabric. If desired, practise first by stamping onto plain white paper. Gently lift off the stamp.

5 Reapply the ink or paint and repeat steps 3 and 4 to print the other flowers. Leave to dry. Wash the stamp and roller immediately.

6 Once the paint is dry, follow the fabric paint manufacturer's instructions to fix the paint. Usually this involves ironing onto the wrong side of the design.

Smudged Stripes

HAND-PAINTED RAINBOW LINES give a new slant to trendy stripes. The bold irregular stripes have an artistic dripping quality that creates movement, rather than static linearity, in the design. You could also work just one or two horizontal or diagonal stripes across the vertical lines to create intersecting planes for added visual interest.

WHAT YOU NEED
- Newspaper
- White long-sleeve T-shirt
- Cardboard
- Plain, non-shiny, paper
- Scissors
- Fabric paints with fine nozzles in assorted colours (here 9 colours were used)
- Iron and ironing board

HOW TO DO IT

1 Cover a flat work surface with newspaper and place the T-shirt on it, front side up. Insert a piece of card, the width and height of the shirt, between the layers.

2 Cut strips of plain paper to measure the length of the shirt. You will need a strip for each painted line.

3 Using one colour of fabric paint, squeeze a line of paint vertically down one long side of the T-shirt, along an outside edge. Lay a strip of paper over the paint, smooth it down with your hand and then carefully lift off the paper. Discard the paper.

4 Repeat step 3 to make stripes in different colours, allowing a gap of approximately 5 cm (2 in) between each one. Take care to use thin strips of paper and work carefully (from right to left if you are right-handed) so previously painted stripes are not smudged.

5 Leave the T-shirt on the flat work surface to dry. Follow the fabric paint manufacturer's instructions to fix the paint; usually this involves ironing onto the wrong side of the design.

Silver Foil '30'

SILVER METALLIC FOIL creates a flash of high-shine against a bright teal-blue background. Make this your all-time most lucky shirt by using your own personal lucky number. The effect can be created on tiny cropped Ts, vests or on slinkier numbers for a Roller Girl from *Boogie Nights* look.

WHAT YOU NEED

- Teal-blue T-shirt
- Cardboard
- Tracing paper and pencil
- Stencil card
- Cutting mat
- Craft knife
- Masking tape
- Tape measure or ruler
- Stencil brush
- Transfer foil glue
- Silver transfer foil
- Plain paper
- Iron and ironing board

HOW TO DO IT

1 Place the T-shirt on a flat work surface. Insert a piece of cardboard inside the shirt to separate the layers.

2 Source numbers from a design book, use a computer font or photocopy numbers you see in a magazine or book and enlarge them to the required size. Here each number measures 15 x 10 cm (6 x 4 in). Trace the outline of the numbers onto tracing paper with pencil, making sure there is enough space between the numbers. Tape the tracing paper, lead side down, onto the stencil card and re-trace over it to transfer the image. Place the stencil card on a cutting mat and cut out the numbers with a craft knife (see page 107). Turn the stencil card over so the numbers read right-side up.

3 Position the stencil on the top centre of the T-shirt. Measure to ensure that the stencil is centred and straight and secure it at each corner with masking tape.

4 Using the stencil brush, dab the glue evenly inside the cut-outs of the stencil. Remove the masking tape and lift off the stencil. Leave the glue to dry until it becomes clear; usually this takes 4 to 8 hours.

5 Place the silver transfer foil, foil side up, over the glue and smooth down. Fix the foil in place by placing plain paper over the foil and pressing with a hot iron (see page 105). Remove the paper to reveal the design.

Purple Foil Love Heart

MAKE AN IMPACT with a simple larger-than-life graphic shape. If a heart doesn't inspire you, try a diamond, flower or star. Foil transfer leaf enables you to mimic the metallic detailing seen on so many shop-bought tops. The foil is worked in a similar way to gilding, with the foil pressed over glue.

Tip
For an extra-glittery design, stitch sequins or apply a thin line of glitter fabric paint around the outline of the shape (see pages 57 and 105).

WHAT YOU NEED
- Deep purple T-shirt
- Cardboard
- Stencil card
- Pencil or pen
- Cutting mat
- Craft knife
- Masking tape
- Tape measure or ruler
- Stencil brush
- Transfer foil glue
- Purple transfer foil
- Plain paper
- Iron and ironing board

HOW TO DO IT
1 Place the T-shirt, front side up, on a flat work surface. Insert a piece of cardboard into the shirt to separate the back and front layers.

2 Cut out a heart stencil. Draw a heart measuring approximately 19 x 22 cm (7½ x 8½ in) onto the stencil card. Alternatively, cut out a paper heart and trace round it onto the stencil card. Cut out the heart stencil using a craft knife and cutting mat (see page 107).

3 Position the stencil on the centre front of the T-shirt. Measure to ensure that the stencil is centred and straight. Secure it at each corner with masking tape.

4 Using the stencil brush, dab the glue into the heart area. Remove the tape and lift off the stencil. Leave the glue to dry for 4 to 8 hours until it is clear.

5 Following the manufacturer's instructions, place the purple transfer foil over the glue and smooth down. Fix the foil by placing plain paper over the foil and pressing with an iron (see page 105). Remove the paper.

Purple
Dalmatian
Spots

WHO LET THE DOGS OUT? Four different sizes of spots are used to create a lively all-over pattern that suggests a Dalmatian's coat. Try black spots on a white background for an authentic look, or go wild and work with multicoloured ink. Team it with jeans for a relaxed but fun look. The technique would work to good effect on skirts, bags, jackets or even on jeans – perhaps randomly placing the spots on the top half and the back pockets of beaten-up distressed jeans.

WHAT YOU NEED
- Newspaper
- Lilac cotton T-shirt
- Cardboard
- Compasses and a pen
- 4 pieces of stencil card
- Cutting mat
- Craft knife
- 'Invisible' or 'fade away' pen fabric marker (optional)
- Stencil brush
- Purple fabric paint
- Iron and ironing board

HOW TO DO IT

1 Cover a flat work surface with newspaper. Place the T-shirt on the work surface and insert a piece of cardboard between the back and front layers.

2 Make stencils for four different-sized spots. Using compasses and a pen, draw each spot onto a separate piece of stencil card (see page 107). Place the cards on a cutting mat and cut out the circles with a craft knife.

3 The spots are randomly placed by working the larger ones first and filling in the empty areas with smaller spots. If you prefer to work out placement first, measure and mark the central positions for the spots with a small dot, using the fabric marker.

4 Position the largest stencil on the T-shirt in the desired position, making sure that the top is smooth and straight. Holding the stencil in place around the edges with your left hand, dab the stencil brush in purple fabric paint with your right hand. Apply the paint to the T-shirt through the cut out circle (see page 107). Do not overload the brush or the paint will seep underneath the stencil. Reapply the paint to the brush, as necessary. Once you have painted the circle, carefully lift off the stencil.

5 Repeat to paint on the other spots, working the largest first, down to the smallest. If the stencil card will overlap onto previously painted spots, allow the paint to dry on those spots before continuing. Wash the stencil brush and stencil cards, if reusing them, immediately.

6 Leave the shirt to dry. When the design is completely dry, follow the fabric paint manufacturer's instructions to fix the paint; usually this involves ironing on the wrong side of the design.

Japanese Blossom

A SINGLE, GRACEFUL STEM of cherry blossom arches across a pistachio-green skirt, creating a tranquil Eastern feel. Keep the look subtle and don't overpower this delicate design with a cacophony of florals or prints. Simply team it with a subtle pink or white T-shirt and flat sandals.

WHAT YOU NEED

- Newspapers
- Masking tape
- Mint green skirt (or try using one in another pastel colour, such as pale blue)
- Cardboard
- 'Invisible' or 'fade away' pen fabric marker
- Fine- and medium-tipped artists' brushes
- Black, pale pink and rose-pink fabric paints
- Iron and ironing board

HOW TO DO IT

1 Cover a flat work surface with newspaper, securing it with tape. Decide whether you want the design on the front or back of the skirt and then place it on the work surface. Insert a piece of cardboard into the skirt to separate the front and back and then tape the skirt to the work surface so that the area you are going to paint is smooth and taut.

2 Draw the blossom branch freehand onto the skirt with the fabric marker. Sketch out the gently tapering branches first, and then add the blossoms on the uppermost branches.

3 Paint the design using the medium-tipped brush for filling in colour and the fine-tipped brush for adding detail. Paint the branch of the blossom first, using black fabric paint. Allow the paint to dry and wash the brush.

4 When the branch is dry, paint the blossom flowers and buds in a pale pink. Add darker rose-pink highlights to the blossoms, softly blending into the wet pale pink colour at the edges. Wash the brushes immediately.

5 Leave the skirt on the flat work surface to dry. Follow the fabric paint manufacturer's instructions to fix the paint; usually this involves ironing onto the wrong side of the design.

Puffa Paint Spots

DECORATE A STRETCHY TOP with spots for an elegant and pretty look. An entirely novel way with spots, these embossed puffs give added texture and detail to a top. Concentrating more spots at the top and spacing them out gradually towards the bottom creates a starry effect, but you could also work them in rows or along seams.

WHAT YOU NEED
- Red sleeveless cotton top
- Cardboard
- Tape measure
- Pink puffa paint with a fine nozzle
- Iron and ironing board

Tip
Try multicoloured dots on white for a more playful approach or work them on a satin bomber jacket for a groovier vibe.

HOW TO DO IT

1 Place the top, front side up, on a flat work surface. Insert a piece of cardboard measuring the width and height of the top between the layers.

2 Squeeze small dots out of the tube of paint onto the shirt. The harder you squeeze, the bigger the dot will be (practise on plain paper first). Here, more dots were randomly placed around the top, with spots gradually dispersing towards the bottom.

3 When you have finished the design, leave the top flat overnight for the paint to dry.

4 Once the paint has dried completely, turn the top inside out and slip it over the end of the ironing board. Iron the front of the top where the dots have been applied. Following the manufacturer's instructions, press the iron down carefully over the spots; do not glide the iron back and forth. The heat will make the painted dots puff up.

Red Leopard

DYING TO MIX WITH the JET-SET? Au sauvage! Get yourself some leopard spots and you'll look the part, whether you are rubbing shoulders with the fashion pack or just aspiring to. Team these vibrant oh-so hot orange spots with black leather trousers and a studded belt and blend in with the celeb crowd. For a more casual look, use the top to spice up military wear.

HOW TO DO IT

1 Cover a flat work surface with newspaper. Place the top on the work surface and insert a piece of cardboard between the back and front layers.

2 Make sure that the top is smooth and straight, then position the leopard stencil on top and secure it to the work surface at each corner with masking tape.

3 Dab the stencil brush in red fabric paint and apply it to the top through the cut-out sections (see page 107). Hold down the edges of the stencil with your other hand if they begin to curl up; this will help to keep the edges crisp. Do not overload the brush or paint will seep underneath the stencil. Reapply the red fabric paint to the brush, as necessary.

4 Once you have painted through the entire stencil, remove the masking tape at the corners and carefully lift off the stencil. Leave the top to dry. Wash the stencil brush and stencil card, if reusing, immediately.

5 Once the front is dry, you can stencil the back of the top, if desired. Simply repeat the steps above.

6 When one, or both, sides of the painted top are dry, follow the fabric paint manufacturer's instructions to fix the paint. Usually this involves ironing onto the wrong side of the design.

WHAT YOU NEED

- Newspaper
- Orange vest top
- Cardboard
- Pre-cut leopard stencil (see resources, page 141)
- Masking tape
- Stencil brush
- Red fabric paint
- Iron and ironing board

Big Pink Spot

WHAT YOU NEED

· Newspaper or an old sheet
  or fabric remnant
· Masking tape
· Orange cotton sweater
· Cardboard
· Plain newspaper
· Compasses, pen and scissors
· Tape measure or ruler
· Screen-printing screen
· Pink water-based
  screen-printing ink
· Squeegee or long piece
  of cardboard

A BRIGHT POP ART SPOT makes a funky fashion statement. The graphic simplicity of the design gives the sweater a more unisex feel. But remember that if you are working on a coloured background, the ink colour may not be pure – avoid green on orange, for example, if you don't want to get a murky brown colour.

HOW TO DO IT

1 Cover a flat work surface with newspaper or an old sheet, securing it to the surface with masking tape. Place the sweater, front side up, on top. Insert cardboard into the sweater to separate the layers.

2 Draw a large circle on a piece of newspaper using the compasses and a pen. Here the circle measures 22 cm (9 in) in diameter. Cut out the circle to make a stencil.

3 Position the newspaper stencil centrally on the front of the sweater. Make sure that the sweater is smoothed flat, then measure to make sure that the stencil is centred and straight. Secure it in place at the corners with masking tape. The rest of the sweater should be covered with newspaper. Place the screen on top.

4 Following the screen-printing instructions, pour the pink printing ink in a line longer than the width of the circle along the top end of the screen.

5 Using the squeegee or a piece of cardboard, and holding the screen down firmly with one hand, carefully scrape the ink from end to end to print the spot on the sweater, using an even, firm action. Dab the squeegee or cardboard to remove any excess ink, then repeat to print over the sweater twice (see page 106).

6 Carefully remove the screen and the paper. Discard the paper and immediately wash the screen and squeegee. Allow the ink to dry for the recommended time . When dry, fix the printed design according to the screen-printing instructions.

Winged 'PETRA' Shirt

IF YOU'D RATHER PLAY RUGBY than teeter around in stilettos, try the tomboy trend. A sporty top with your name on it can be paired with jeans for a relaxed weekend outfit. If you like the style, but are a true girl at heart, create the letters on a tiny T-shirt and wear with a pretty designer skirt for a street-cool meets *haute couture* look.

WHAT YOU NEED

- Photocopies of letters
- Felt-tip pens
- Scissors
- White paper
- Orange T-shirt
- Tape measure or ruler

HOW TO DO IT

1 The letters here were designed using computer software and were printed out in colour, but you can take black-and-white photocopies of copyright-free typography and colour the letters in using felt-tip pens.

2 Cut out the letters. Place a piece of paper on the shirt and arrange the letters in a slightly curved formation. Measure to ensure the letters are straight and equally spaced. The first and last letters should be at the same level, and at the same distance from the side seams. Take a colour copy of the paper with the letters in place.

3 Take the photocopy to a copy shop or T-shirt printer that offers colour transfers on fabric and have the image printed directly onto the front of the shirt.

Alarm Clock Print

FOR ALL THOSE DESIGN JUNKIES out there, imprint an image of your favourite piece of technology onto your sweatshirt. This digital alarm clock may be just the type of design you love, or try a state-of-the-art image like a computer mouse or mobile (cell) phone, or go for nostalgic retro designs, such as an old-fashioned dial telephone.

WHAT YOU NEED

- Copyright-free image of an alarm clock or other gadget
- Pink felt-tip pen
- Grey sweatshirt

HOW TO DO IT

1 Using a copyright-free design, make a black-and-white photocopy of a picture of an alarm clock. Colour in the figures with a pink felt-tip pen to resemble the fluorescent read-out of a digital clock.

2 Take the photocopy to a copy shop or T-shirt printer that offers colour transfers on fabric. Have the copy shop or T-shirt printer transfer-print the image directly onto the front of the sweatshirt.

Cat and Dog
Print T-shirts

KEEP YOUR LOOK CUTE and kitsch with these T-shirts, which would also make a great gift. Pay homage to a well-loved pet by featuring your own dog or cat on the shirt. You can use a single colour, assorted colours or two alternating colours of gemstones to frame your animal picture.

WHAT YOU NEED

- Photocopy of your pet cat or dog (or any other animal)
- Scissors
- Coloured T-shirt
- Chalk or pen fabric marker
- Strong fabric glue
- 18 flat-backed gemstones in colours of your choice
- Tweezers

HOW TO DO IT

1 Make a colour photocopy of a cat or dog on a coloured background. Alternatively, if you have a computer and a scanner, scan a photograph of your pet into your computer and use your software to create a background frame for the image, before printing out the image from a colour printer. Take your image to a copy shop or T-shirt printer that offers colour transfers. Ask the shop to transfer-print the design directly onto the front of your T-shirt. Some photography developers can even transfer-print images taken from your own photographs onto T-shirts.

2 Place the printed T-shirt, image side up, on a flat work surface. With the fabric marker, mark equally spaced positions for the gemstones around the frame of the design. Working one gemstone at a time, place a dab of glue on a marked position and carefully stick a gemstone in place using tweezers. Leave the shirt flat until the glue is dry.

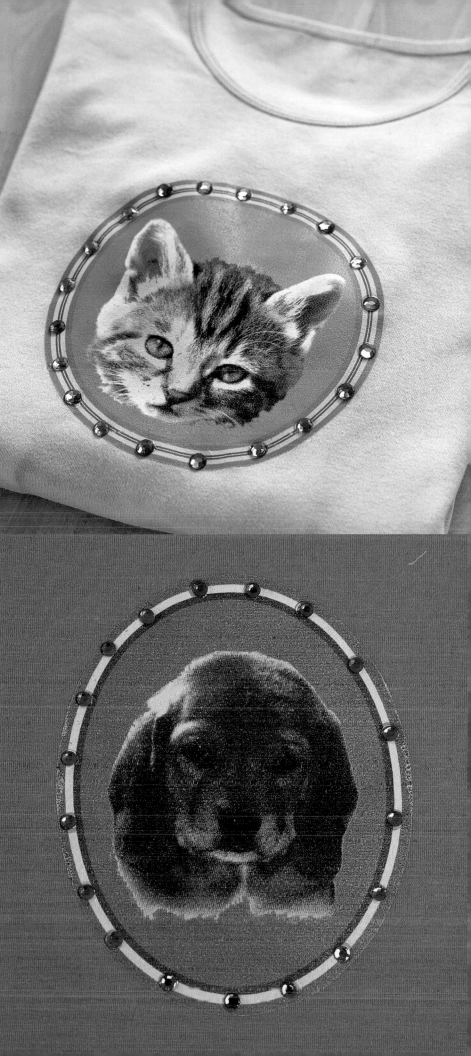

Glitter Flower

The OUTLINE of a gigantic flower head, depicted in glitter and standing out in sharp relief from a dark background, makes a dramatic statement. Use a stylized profile of a just-opening bloom and work the design in the bottom corner of the shirt, with the stamens spraying outwards. The glitter flower adds feminine appeal to an army-green T-shirt. Combine it with camouflage trousers and wear your hair in a rockabilly quiff (coif) for that happening butch look.

WHAT YOU NEED
- Newspapers
- Olive green sleeveless cotton T-shirt
- Cardboard
- Masking tape
- 'Invisible' or 'fade away' pen fabric marker
- Strong fabric glue with a thin nozzle
- Fine washable glitter in pink

HOW TO DO IT

1 Cover a flat work surface with newspaper. Place the T-shirt on the work surface and insert a piece of cardboard, measuring the size of the design, between the back and front layers. Secure the T-shirt to the work surface with masking tape around the edges of the cardboard so that the shirt's surface is smooth and taut.

2 Draw the design of the flower freehand on the front of the T-shirt with the fabric marker. This design was inspired by an image from a flower book.

3 Practise squeezing out the fabric glue before you start; apply consistent pressure so that the glue comes out in a thin, even stream. Trace over the design with the glue and immediately sprinkle on the pink glitter. There should be a heavy coating of glitter, without any glue showing through. Leave to dry overnight.

4 When dry, shake off the excess glitter onto newspaper to reveal the design.

Leaf-Print

A LUSH COLLAGE of foliage and flowers has an organic feel. Shades of green conjure up an oasis of calm, and you will feel completely chilled when wearing this top. If green's not your colour, choose another motif, such as roses or orchids on a dusty pink shirt.

WHAT YOU NEED

- Green long-sleeved T-shirt
- Colour photocopies of leaves and flowers (copyright-free)
- Scissors
- White paper
- Glue

HOW TO DO IT

1 Cut out the leaf and flower shapes. Place the T-shirt on a flat work surface and place the white paper over the top. Arrange the shapes on the front until you are pleased with the design and their position on the T-shirt and then glue them in place. Take a colour photocopy of the paper with the leaves and flowers in place.

2 Take the photocopy of the finished design to a copy shop or T-shirt printer that offers colour transfers and ask them to transfer-print the design directly onto your T-shirt in your chosen position.

Glitter Heart Pockets

Draw attention to your derrière with these sparkly hearts. Almost any other motif would work – think Evisu jeans for an abstract design, or use glittering stars. For a more suggestive look, substitute right and left hands for the hearts and work them in a larger size on the back of a pocketless skirt.

WHAT YOU NEED
- Newspapers
- Denim skirt
- Stencil card, tracing paper, pencil, cutting mat and craft knife, or a pre-cut heart stencil
- Tape measure or ruler
- Masking tape
- Stencil brush
- Strong fabric glue for glitter
- Fine washable glitter in blue

HOW TO DO IT

1 Cover a flat work surface with newspaper. Place the skirt, front side down, on the work surface and smooth it so the fabric is taut.

2 If you are cutting your own stencil, draw a heart onto the stencil card. Alternatively, cut out a paper heart and trace round it onto the stencil card. Place the stencil card on a cutting mat and cut out the heart with a craft knife to make the stencil (see page 107).

3 Centre the heart stencil on one of the back pockets. Measure to ensure it is centred and straight and secure it in place with masking tape on each corner.

4 Using the stencil brush, dab the fabric glue into the heart area. Immediately sprinkle on the blue glitter. There should be a heavy coating of glitter, without any glue showing through. Remove the masking tape and carefully lift off the stencil.

5 Repeat steps 3 and 4 on the other pocket and wash the stencil brush. Leave to dry for a few hours, preferably overnight, then shake off the excess glitter onto newspaper to reveal the hearts.

Silver Leopard

WHAT YOU NEED
- Pale pink cotton sweatshirt
- Cardboard
- Pre-cut leopard-print stencil
- Masking tape
- 'Invisible' or 'fade away' pen fabric marker
- Fine-tipped artists' brush
- Transfer foil glue
- Silver transfer foil
- Plain paper
- Iron and ironing board

THIS MUST-HAVE SWEATSHIRT has just that key retro shape and the metallic silver offers a high-glam version of leopardskin. Dress it street-gang and tough with a jean skirt or hipsters and a dangling chain belt, or go for the girlie look by mixing it with a sugar-almond or candy-stripe skirt.

HOW TO DO IT

1 Place the sweatshirt, front up, on a flat work surface. Insert a piece of cardboard measuring the width and height of the shirt to separate the back and front layers.

2 Position the stencil over the top, making sure that the sweatshirt is smooth. Secure the stencil to the work surface at each corner with masking tape.

3 Working on one section at a time, use a fine-tipped paintbrush to apply glue into each shape through the stencil. Do not decorate the sleeves or the band around the bottom of the sweatshirt. Remove the tape and lift off the stencil.

4 Leave the glue to dry for the recommended time, usually 4 to 8 hours, until the glue becomes clear.

5 Following the manufacturer's instructions, place the silver transfer foil, foil side up, over the glue and smooth down. Fix the foil in place by placing plain paper over the foil and pressing with a hot iron (see page 105). Remove the paper and the foil will stick to only the glued sections.

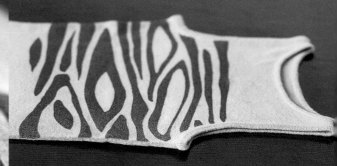

Pink Zebra Print

MAKE IT INTO THE A-LIST with this cool zebra-print top that will transform you from working girl to lounge lizard. Pink animal-skin prints are all the rage on the catwalk, so you are up there with the best. You will need to be a dab hand with the pen and scissors to draw and cut out the stencil, but you could also photocopy a design and use it as the basis to create your own.

WHAT YOU NEED

- Newspaper or an old sheet or fabric remnant
- Masking tape
- Camel-coloured wool vest (tank) top
- Cardboard
- Plain newsprint
- Pen or pencil
- Scissors
- Screen-printing screen
- Squeegee or long piece of cardboard
- Pink screen-printing ink, compatible with wool (oil-based)

HOW TO DO IT

1 Cover a flat work surface with newspaper or an old sheet, securing it to the surface with masking tape. Place the vest (tank) top, front side up, on the surface. Insert a piece of cardboard inside the vest top to separate the back and front layers.

2 Draw a zebra design onto a piece of plain newsprint that measures a little larger than the top. First draw around the outline of the top so that you have a guideline for the outline of the design. Draw in ribbing or seam finishes, such as those around the arms or neckline, which you do not want to print. Then draw on the zebra stripes and patterns. If you want the edges to bleed off the sides of the top, extend the drawing outside the outline. To make cutting out the design easier, shade in the areas you want to print with a felt-tip pen or pencil. Cut out the blackened-in areas with scissors to make the zebra-print stencil.

3 Position the newspaper stencil over the front of the top, aligning it with your drawn marks, and secure it in place with masking tape. Make sure that the top is smooth and straight and the stencil is positioned as you like. Any areas you do not want to print should be covered with plain newsprint. Place the screen-printing screen on top of the stencil.

4 Following the screen-printing instructions, pour the pink printing ink along the top end of the screen.

5 Using the squeegee or a piece of cardboard, and holding the screen down firmly with one hand, scrape the ink from end to end to print the design onto the top, using an even, firm action. Dab the squeegee or cardboard to remove excess ink, and repeat to print over the design twice (see page 106).

6 Carefully remove the screen and the newsprint. Discard the newsprint and immediately wash the screen and squeegee. Allow the ink to dry for the recommended time . When dry, fix the printed design according to the screen-printing instructions.

How-to Techniques

BOTH THE TECHNIQUES shown here use a freehand method of painting a design in glue, though one is completed in glitter and the other in iron-on transfer foil. Transfer foils enable a multitude of effects, from a scattering of small dots to a big foil heart, star or number. Because the foil is available in different colours, you have many more choices than simply gold or silver – try multicoloured spots or layer self-colours, such as a metallic blue against a blue fabric, to enhance the contrast of textures.

GLUEING GLITTER

1 Squeeze the glue over the fabric in a thin, even stream to create an abstract pattern. Use a glue that is compatible with the glitter and the same brand.

2 While the glue is still wet, sprinkle on a generous amount of fine machine-washable glitter. Make sure that no glue shows through.

3 Leave the glue to dry for several hours, preferably overnight. When dry, shake off the excess glitter onto paper to reveal the design. The glitter can be reused.

PRINTING FOIL

1 Paint the design freehand onto the fabric using a fabric glue that is compatible with and the same brand as the transfer foil. Leave for 4 to 8 hours, until the glue becomes clear.

2 Place the transfer foil, foil side up, over the glued area and smooth down. Fix the foil by placing plain paper on top and ironing over the design with smooth strokes.

3 Let the design cool for a few minutes and then peel off the paper to reveal the design. The foil will stick only to the glued area.

How-to Techniques

PRINTING TECHNIQUES enable a uniformity of design. Rubber stamping is one of the easiest methods for printing a repeat motif, and it can be used on soft furnishings as well as clothing. Though screen printing seems tricky, once you master it you can print many copies of a design; it is a good way to print T-shirts (as well as flyers or posters) for a club or organization.

SCREEN PRINTING

1 Draw the shape you want to print onto a piece of plain newsprint and cut it out to make a stencil. Position the stencil in place on the garment. Place the screen on top.

2 Pour screen-printing paint in a line along the top end of the screen to the width of the design and about 5 cm (2 in) above the stencil, following the paint instructions.

RUBBER STAMPING

1 Pour or squeeze a small amount of the paint onto a flat plate or tile. Roll the foam roller in the paint. Roll the roller evenly over the rubber stamp to transfer the paint.

3 Holding the squeegee at a 45-degree angle, scrape the paint from end to end. Dab the squeegee to remove excess paint, add more paint if needed, and repeat.

4 Carefully lift off the screen and remove the stencil. Allow the ink to dry for the recommended time . When dry, fix the printed design according to the instructions.

2 Press the stamp down onto the fabric. Do not coat the stamp with too much paint or else the detail will be lost; do not use too little paint, or the design will be faint.

How-to Techniques

STENCILS ARE NECESSARY for many decorative crafts, but once made, they can be reused for different medias if cleaned and stored properly. To make a stencil, use a pen or marker to draw around a template, or draw an image freehand, onto a piece of stencil card, leaving a margin of 7 cm (2 ¾ in) around the edge. If the design is highly detailed, colour in the areas to be cut out with a black felt-tip pen. Place the stencil card on a cutting mat and cut out the shape using a craft knife.

STENCILLING WITH GLITTER

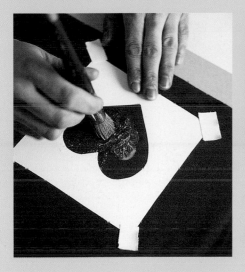

1 Position the stencil on the garment and secure it in place with masking tape on each corner. Dab the stencil brush in the fabric glitter glue and dab inside the stencil.

2 Sprinkle the machine-washable glitter over the glue while it is still wet. Allow the glue to dry for several hours, preferably overnight.

3 When dry, remove the masking tape, carefully lift off the stencil, and shake off the excess glitter onto paper. The extra glitter can be reused for another project.

STENCILLING WITH FABRIC PAINT

1 Position the stencil on the garment and secure it with masking tape on each corner. Dab a stencil brush in the fabric paint sparingly and dab inside the cut-out areas.

2 When the design is painted, remove the masking tape and carefully lift off the stencil, taking care not to smudge the paint. Allow the paint to dry for the recommended time.

5

Dyeing & Bleaching

Learning to add and take away colour from fabric allows you to achieve a huge range of effects and opens up a whole world of textile design. A word of warning: whether you are tie-dyeing or bleaching, you need to protect surfaces and your skin. Once you have flicked bleach onto a garment, or dyed a white T-shirt pink, there will be no turning back. If desired, experiment on a fabric scrap first.

Spattered T-shirt

WEAR YOUR ART ON YOUR SLEEVE. An olive green T-shirt dabbled and spattered with bleach and paint says you are an artist with attitude. In the manner of Jackson Pollock, gesture and action is involved in creating this abstract design. So experiment with bold splashes of bleach broken by intricate laceworks of paint dribbling to create your own highly individualistic work of art.

WHAT YOU NEED

- Newspapers
- Olive green T-shirt
- 2 pieces of cardboard
- Rubber gloves
- Bleach
- Dark green fabric paint
- Paintbrushes in various sizes
- Iron and ironing board

HOW TO DO IT

1 Cover a flat work surface with newspaper. As this project involves flicking bleach, do the design outdoors if at all possible.

2 Make sure the T-shirt is clean and dry. Place a large piece of cardboard inside to separate the front and back, and place the shirt flat on the covered surface. Wear old clothes and rubber gloves to protect your skin.

3 Using different sizes of paintbrush, flick bleach over the T-shirt to create patterns. Use a quick sharp action of the wrist and allow the bleach to soak in a little after each flicking action, as it will spread slightly. Leave the T-shirt for 20 minutes to allow the bleach to soak in. Immediately wash the brushes.

4 Machine wash and dry the T shirt.

5 Re-cover the work surface with fresh newspaper. When the T-shirt is dry, place a new piece of cardboard inside it and place it on the work surface. Using a smaller, clean paintbrush, flick dark green fabric paint over the T-shirt. Leave to dry.

6 Once the paint is dry, follow the fabric paint manufacturer's instructions to fix the paint. Usually this involves ironing on the wrong side of the design.

Bleached Crossed Heart

A HEART MOTIF, ETCHED IN BLEACH, has a stark simplicity on a plain vivid-coloured background. The heart is slightly crossed at the bottom to create a more stylized image. You could create other graffiti-like symbols or drawings, such as stick figures, noughts-and-crosses (tic-tac-toe), abstract squiggles or swirls, or brushwork a name on the shirt, like Stephen Sprouse did for Louis Vuitton.

WHAT YOU NEED

- Green top
- Cardboard
- Paper
- Scissors
- Pin
- Tape measure
- Fine-tipped artists' brush
- Bleach
- Rubber gloves

HOW TO DO IT

1 Place the top on a flat work surface and insert a piece of cardboard inside to separate the back and front.

2 Cut a heart to the desired size from paper to use as a template. Position the heart template on the front of the top with a pin, measuring to ensure that it is centred and straight.

3 Using the paintbrush and bleach, carefully hand-paint the heart around the template. Immediately wash the brush after use.

4 Once the bleach heart has appeared, after about 20 minutes, wash and dry the top.

Bleached and Dyed
Pink-Black Jeans

WITH THE CURRENT TREND to trash running at fever pitch in fashion design, try your hand at distressing and 'destroying' a pair of jeans. A key look that went from street to catwalk, bleached jeans are given a new twist here by adding in colour with pink dye. The dye adds a tonal depth, while giving a splash of colour to the bleached areas, creating a cutting-edge effect that will appeal to the most die-hard trend-setter.

WHAT YOU NEED

- Newspapers
- Black denim jeans
- Bleach
- Various paintbrushes, including a 5 cm- (2 in-) decorating brush
- Rubber gloves
- Pink hand or machine dye
- Salt, or other recommended fixative
- Plastic bucket (if hand-dyeing)

HOW TO DO IT

1 As this project involves painting with bleach, work outdoors if possible, and wear old clothes and rubber gloves to protect your skin. Cover a flat work surface with newspaper and place the jeans on it, front sides up.

2 Paint and dribble the bleach over the jeans to create abstract patterns. Here deep splashes of bleach were made at the hem with finer sprays and flicks at the top. Once the bleach has been absorbed, after about 40 minutes, turn the jeans over and repeat on the other side.

3 When all the bleached design has been revealed, thoroughly wash the jeans, but do not dry them.

4 Following the dye manufacturer's instructions, dye the jeans pink by hand or in the washing machine. You will need to use a quantity of fixative, such as salt, depending on the weight of the fabric and according to the instructions.

5 After the specified time, rinse well, and then wash and air-dry the jeans.

Tie-dye
or Die

Take a long look back with this classic tie-dye treatment. A throwback to the 1970s made contemporary, think Venice Beach skateboarder or Malibu surfer for this laid-back casual wear. The size of circles you make depends on how much fabric you gather in bunches; if you want to make circles within circles, tie an extra elastic band around the top of each bunch. The pale blue colour is subtle and soft, but for more visual punch, dye the shirt bright purple or orange.

WHAT YOU NEED
- Long-sleeve white or cream T-shirt
- Pale blue hand or machine dye
- Salt, or other recommended fixative
- 5 mm- (¼ in-) wide elastic bands
- Plastic bucket (if hand-dyeing)
- Rubber gloves

HOW TO DO IT
1 Pre-wash the T-shirt according to the label's instructions, but do not dry.

2 While the T-shirt is still damp, tie two elastic bands at even intervals on each sleeve. Pinch a little fabric from the front of the T-shirt and attach an elastic band about 5 cm (2 in) from the top of the bunch. The further away from the top you attach the elastic, the larger the circle will be. Continue tying bunches of fabric over the front and back of the T-shirt.

3 Following the dye manufacturer's instructions, dye the shirt by hand in a plastic bucket or in the washing machine. You will need to use a quantity of fixative, such as salt, depending on the weight of the fabric and according to the instructions.

4 After the specified time, rinse the T-shirt well several times, and remove the elastic bands to reveal the pattern. Wash, dry and press the T-shirt.

Red & Pink
Tie-dye shirt

An edging of twinkling pink sequins glows against a subtle striped background, created from muted bands of pink and red dye. Red has made a big comeback, and being more vibrant and harder-edged than the shades of pink seen everywhere, it is a great colour to add full-on sexiness to a look, or to team with jeans.

WHAT YOU NEED

- White cotton thermal shirt
- Red hand dye
- Pink hand dye
- Salt, or other recommended fixative
- 2 plastic buckets
- Rubber gloves
- 5mm- (¼in) thick elastic bands
- Tape measure
- Pink sequin trim
- Pins
- Scissors
- Pink sewing thread
- Sewing needle

HOW TO DO IT

1 Pre-wash the thermal shirt according to the label's instructions, but do not dry. Then, following the dye manufacturer's instructions, prepare the red dye and pink dye with the fixative in separate buckets.

2 While the shirt is still damp, tie elastic bands around the body (but not the sleeves) at varying intervals. If you want the stripes to be even, measure the intervals at which you tie the bands to make sure they are all the same measurement.

3 First dye the thermal shirt in the red dye, leaving it to soak for the recommended time. Rinse well and remove the elastic bands.

4 Now dye the shirt in the pink dye, leaving it to soak for the recommended time. Remove from the dye bath and rinse well. Wash, dry and press the shirt.

5 Measure the circumference of the neckline and cut a length of sequin trim to size, adding 1 cm (½ in).

6 Pin the sequin trim to the neckline, overlapping the short ends neatly at a side shoulder seam to join. Hand-sew in place using a running stitch and the pink thread, following the centre stitching of the trim.

Black
Spotty
T-shirt

A SIMPLE BLACK-AND-WHITE spotted shirt is dyed and embellished with a bow to match a pair of shoes. The pretty scoop-neck top would look ladylike and grown-up when teamed with a black pencil or pleated skirt. Alternatively, take a tip from Chloe Sevigny and think outside the box, perhaps teaming the top with slouchy pinstripe hipsters or a frilly vintage skirt.

WHAT YOU NEED
- White cotton shirt with black spots
- Pale blue hand or machine dye
- Salt, or other recommended fixative
- Plastic bucket (if hand-dyeing)
- Rubber gloves
- 5 mm- (¼in-) wide black velvet ribbon, about 20 cm (8 in) long
- Black sewing thread
- Sewing needle

HOW TO DO IT
1 Pre-wash the shirt according to the shirt's label instructions. Then, following the dye manufacturer's instructions, dye the shirt by hand in a plastic bucket or in the washing machine. You will need to use a quantity of fixative, such as salt, depending on the weight of the fabric and according to the instructions.

2 After the specified time, rinse well several times, and then wash, dry and press the shirt.

3 Tie the black velvet ribbon in a bow. Hand-sew the bow to the centre front of the shirt using a few slipstitches and the black thread.

Velvet
Spotty Skirt

CLEMENTS RIBEIRO DOESN'T HAVE a monopoly on spots. Here super-sized spots are first created with bleach and then dyed to create a graphic effect that is fresh, fun and far removed from prissy polka dots. This uniquely exuberant design needs to be worn with panache, perhaps by pairing it with brightly coloured fishnets or ankle socks and heels.

WHAT YOU NEED

- Newspapers
- Beige or neutral coloured velvet skirt
- Cardboard
- Bleach
- Paintbrush
- Rubber gloves
- Compasses, pen, cardboard and scissors or craft knife
- Turquoise dye
- Salt, or other recommended fixative
- Plastic bucket

HOW TO DO IT

1 Cover a flat work surface with newspaper. Make sure the skirt is clean and dry. Place a large piece of cardboard inside to separate the front and back, and place the skirt flat on the covered surface. Wear old clothes and rubber gloves to protect your skin.

2 Paint the spots freehand on the skirt with the bleach. Alternatively, use compasses and pen to draw a circle onto cardboard and cut out the circle to make a stencil. Position the stencil on the skirt and paint in the circle with bleach. Here the spots were made using the freehand method and they all vary in size.

3 Once you have painted the spots on the front of the skirt, turn the skirt over and paint more spots on the back of the skirt.

4 Air-dry the skirt on a washing line to allow the bleach to absorb for about 40 minutes.

5 When the spots are clearly revealed, thoroughly wash the skirt, but do not dry it.

6 Following the dye manufacturer's instructions, prepare a turquoise dye bath and dye the skirt by hand in a plastic bucket. You will need to use a quantity of fixative, such as salt, depending on the weight of the fabric and according to the instructions.

7 After the specified time, rinse well several times, and then hand-wash and air-dry the skirt.

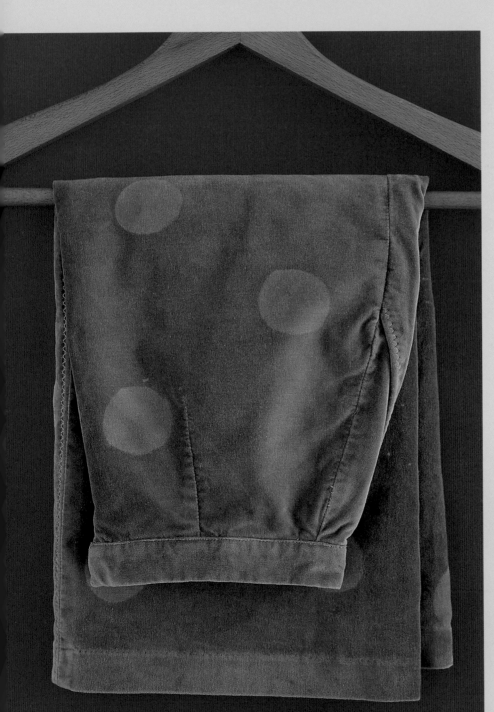

Dip-dyed
White Tanks

CREATE THESE ALMOST ROTHKO-LIKE colour blocks that bleed and blur at the edges by simply dipping white tops in coloured dye. The sharp, unexpected contrast of colour against white makes a uniquely artistic design. For a more saturated and dramatic effect, try layering colours by dyeing the top a lighter colour first, such as pink or yellow, and then dip-dyeing in a stronger colour, such as red or orange.

WHAT YOU NEED

- 2 white tank tops
- Red and purple hand dye, or colours of your choice
- Salt, or other recommended fixative
- Plastic bucket
- Rubber gloves
- Washing powder (detergent)

HOW TO DO IT

1 Pre-wash the tank tops according to the label's instructions. Then, following the dye manufacturer's instructions, prepare different-colour dye baths in separate plastic buckets. You will need to use a quantity of fixative, such as salt, depending on the weight of the fabric and according to the instructions.

2 Dip each tank top into the dye as far as you want the dye to go. Hold in the dye until the colour is several shades deeper than the one you want.

3 Ring out the excess dye and hand-wash only the area that has been dyed with washing powder (detergent), following the dye manufacturer's instructions. Hang the tank tops up to dry.

Candy-coloured Cardigans

Tip

Don't be afraid to go for juicy lemon, orange or lime colours, and a cardigan can be dyed to match a favourite skirt or dress in a splashy fluoro floral. The dye colour will be less saturated on the lace trim.

THESE LACE-TRIMMED CARDIGANS, one pretty in pink and the other Côte d'Azur blue, are perfect accessories for summery slip dresses. Whether you are a girl-about-town or holidaying in Barbados, the lightweight cardigans will keep the chill off your shoulders.

WHAT YOU NEED

- 2 white or cream thermal cotton cardigans
- Turquoise and pink hand or machine dye
- Salt, or other recommended fixative
- 2 plastic buckets (if hand-dyeing)
- Rubber gloves
- Felt flower brooch
- Tape measure
- 15mm- ($^5/_8$in-) wide green velvet ribbon trim
- Scissors
- Sewing machine
- Pins
- Green sewing thread

HOW TO DO IT

1 Pre-wash the cardigans according to the label's instructions. Then, following the dye manufacturer's instructions, dye the cardigans by hand in separate plastic buckets or in the washing machine. You will need to use a quantity of fixative, such as salt, depending on the weight of the fabric.

2 After the specified time, rinse well several times, and then wash, dry and press the cardigans.

3 Pin the brooch on the upper left corner of the turquoise cardigan.

4 For the pink cardigan, add the velvet green trim. Place the cardigan on a flat surface and measure round the circumference of the cuffs and hem. Cut three lengths of velvet ribbon to size, adding an extra 1 cm (½ in) to each length.

5 Pin the velvet trim to the edge of the cuffs, flush with the edge of the lace trim. Turn under one short end and overlap onto the other at the seam to join. Pin the length of trim for the hem on in the same way, but position 1 cm (½in) inside the edge of the hem. Measure to ensure the velvet trim is straight.

6 Using the green thread and a straight stitch, machine-stitch each length of velvet trim in place. Work as close to the edge as possible and stitch along both long sides of the velvet.

Bleach-splattered Denim Skirt

Tip
Experiment with splashes, flicks, spots, dribbles, swirls and circles of bleach on a denim remnant before deciding which methods to use. Gold or silver fabric paint or broken patches of metallic transfer foil add cool detailing to bleached denim.

WHAT YOU NEED
· Newspapers
· Denim skirt
· Cardboard
· Bleach
· Rubber gloves

HOW TO DO IT

1 Cover a flat work surface with newspaper. As this project involves dribbling with bleach, do the design outdoors if at all possible. Place the skirt on the work surface and insert a piece of cardboard inside to separate the front and back layers. Wear rubber gloves and old clothes to protect your skin.

2 Dribble the bleach straight from the container onto the skirt to create an abstract pattern. Here an almost linear design was created by slowly pouring thin streams of bleach over the skirt. Allow the bleach to absorb for 20 minutes. Turn the skirt over and repeat on the other side. Leave for another 20 minutes.

3 Once the bleach effect is fully revealed, thoroughly wash and air-dry the skirt.

Wiggle-
print Skirt

DRIBBLES AND SPLASHES of bleach create a painterly effect on a blue denim skirt that is highly individualistic and expressionistic – no one else will have one quite like yours. Go for the flashy-trashy trailer-park look and decorate it with squiggles of pink fabric paint. Wear it funky and offbeat with a bomber jacket or striped zip-up, or glam it up like L'il Kim with gold chains, belts and ankle boots.

WHAT YOU NEED

- Newspapers
- Denim skirt
- Cardboard
- Bleach
- Rubber gloves
- Pink fabric paint in a tube with a thin nozzle
- Plain, not shiny, white paper
- Iron and ironing board

HOW TO DO IT

1 Repeat steps 1, 2 and 3 of Bleach-splattered Denim Skirt (left) to dribble or splash a bleach pattern onto a denim skirt.

2 Once the skirt is dry, cover a flat work surface with newspaper. Place the skirt on the work surface and insert a piece of cardboard inside to separate the layers.

3 Squeeze the tube of paint directly onto the skirt to create a wiggly abstract design. If desired, practise on paper first to get a feel for the pressure you need to apply the squiggles.

4 Lay a piece of paper over the paint and smudge the paint by gently smoothing your fingers over the paper. You will need a clean piece of paper for each area you smudge. Allow the paint to dry.

5 When dry, turn the skirt over and repeat steps 3 and 4 on the other side.

6 Once the paint is dry, follow the fabric paint manufacturer's instructions to fix the paint. Usually this involves ironing onto the wrong side of the fabric.

How-to Techniques

ALTHOUGH TIE-DYEING is a familiar technique for most people, it is often an inexact science – however, sometimes the unexpected yields the best results. Be bold with your tying techniques if you feel the ones shown here are too simplistic, but do get to know colours and how they mix. As a general rule, dye with darker colours first, using progressively lighter dyes as you work.

BASIC TIE-DYEING

1 To create circular designs on a shirt, pinch a little fabric on a damp 100% cotton shirt and secure with an elastic band. Repeat all over the shirt. The more fabric you pinch, the larger the circle will be.

2 To create stripes, tie elastic bands at varying intervals around a damp 100% cotton shirt. If you want even stripes, measure the intervals at which you tie the bands to make sure they are all the same.

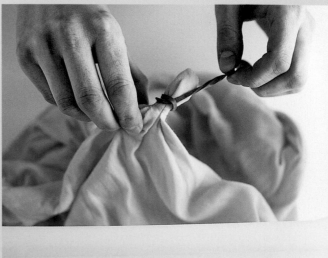

3 Prepare a dye bath according to the dye instructions. You will need to dissolve the dye and fixative in a bucket of warm water. Dip the garment into the dye and allow to soak for the recommended time.

4 Squeeze the excess dye from the garment and rinse well several times under cold water. Remove the elastic bands to reveal the design and hang the garment up to dry.

How-to Techniques

BLEACH IS A LOT MORE ADAPTABLE to painterly expression than you might think. Bold haphazard splashes of reverse-dyed fabric are not the only option; bleaching techniques can be controlled and meticulous too. Delicate line etchings in bleach can give clothing an intricate pictorial quality, and here are techniques for detailed work as well as for expressionistic and abstract designs.

POURING BLEACH

5 Here is one of the many colour effects that can be created using tie-dyeing techniques, as shown left.

1 To create more abstract designs, simply pour liquid household bleach on the surface of fabric. Only use bleach on 100% cotton fabrics, wear rubber gloves, and protect surrounding surfaces.

PRINTING WITH BLEACH

1 Pour a small amount of liquid household bleach into a plastic bowl. Dip a paintbrush into the bleach and paint the design onto the fabric as if you were using paint.

6

Accessories

Whether it is a bag, belt or hairslide, an accessory can change the look of an outfit, and is guaranteed to grab attention. How satisfying when you can say that it is one of your own creations! Most of the techniques used in the previous chapters can be applied to accessories. Bleach and stud denim bags, or insert gemstones into a striped mesh tote. Hats, too, are endlessly adaptable.

Corsage
Choker

THIS SEXY BLACK-AND-RED CHOKER lends an air of mystery and haunting beauty to a look. For a different alternative, though, think frou-frou 1950s proms with pale orchids or frilly flowers in delicate pastel shades of lilac, pink or lemon meringue. Whatever colours you choose, keep other accessories to the minimum. The flower will be your focal point, so avoid hair accessories and anything but the simplest earrings. Hair swept off the face and neck also suits the style.

WHAT YOU NEED

- Tape measure
- Scissors
- 3.5 cm- (1⅓ in-) wide black velvet ribbon
- Sew-on Velcro
- Black thread
- Sewing needle
- Red fabric flower (or another colour of your choice)

HOW TO DO IT

1 Measure around your neck with a tape measure and add an extra 4 cm (1½ in) to the final measurement. Cut a length of velvet ribbon to size. Fold over and press each short end by 1 cm (½ in).

2 Cut a short piece of Velcro, slightly less than the width of the ribbon and about 1 cm (½ in) long.

3 Velcro has two sides: the hook side and the loop side. Hand-sew or machine-stitch the hook side to one end of the velvet ribbon, on the right side. Check the fit to make sure the ends will overlap neatly before sewing the loop side to the other end, but on the wrong side of the ribbon. The loop side of Velcro should overlap the hook side.

4 Fold the ribbon in half lengthways to find the front centre. Hand-sew the flower onto the centre at this point using tiny stitches to secure. Alternatively, and especially if the flower is large, sew the flower on to one side of the velvet ribbon to sit just under the jawline.

Sage Corsage on Zebra-print

A SAGE-COLOURED FLOWER softens the striking prints on this zebra-print top. While almost any accent colour looks good with black and white, such as scarlet, hot pink, orange and turquoise, try using softer hues against this strong pattern for a more subtle approach. Teal, lilac, peach, sugar pink or baby blue will all work well. Don't worry about the colour being lost against the background – pretty flowers are always noticeable! You can use huge camellias or full-blown roses or even a tiny cluster of pansies grouped together. For that *Sex and the City* look, pin a gigantic flower head on the shoulder of a slinky one-strap top.

WHAT YOU NEED
· Sage-green paper or fabric flower
· Brooch pin
· Clear 'invisible' thread and needle, or
· Strong contact glue
· Zebra-print top

HOW TO DO IT

1 Hand-sew a brooch pin onto the reverse of the flower. To make the first knot, run the thread through the pin and into the flower, leaving a little extra thread hanging. Knot the thread tightly to the hanging end, and then continue to sew, wrapping the thread round the brooch pin as you work along the length. Repeat the knot at the opposite end.

2 Alternatively attach the flower to the pin back with a strong contact glue and allow to dry.

3 Place the top on a flat work surface and pin the corsage on the upper left side. Depending on the type of top, you can pin the corsage at the décolletage, at the waist, or even on handbags, belts, lapels, hats and scarves, or pin it on an ankle strap of your favourite sandals (only do one though – two is overkill).

Stripy Scarf with Appliqué Handbag

STRIPES CONTINUE TO BE A BIG TREND, appearing on the catwalk in all guises. A jolly striped scarf trimmed with fun, whimsical motifs will bring out the child in you. Try to find a scarf in as many colours as possible – you can then wear it with everything you own! If you are not so keen on the handbag idea, try making a colourful teapot, farm animal or even a little person with yarn hair who looks exactly like you to sew on the scarf.

WHAT YOU NEED

- Ready-made scarf in striped felted wool, measuring 100 x 22 cm (39 x 8½ in)
- Two 26 cm- (10 in-) lengths pink pom-pom trim
- Scissors
- Pins
- Sewing needle
- Beading needle
- Pink, turquoise and yellow thread
- Scraps of pale blue thick felted wool
- Scrap turquoise craft felt
- Fabric glue
- Short length pink sequin trim
- Button
- 9 round pink beads
- 2 turquoise glass bugle beads
- 4 cm- (1½ in-) length pink cord
- 9 cm- (3½ in-) length orange metallic cord

HOW TO DO IT

1 Along each short edge of the scarf, pin on the pom-pom trim, so the pom-poms hang over the edge. Turn under the raw edges on each side to neatly align with the edge of the scarf. Hand-sew in place with pink thread, using a running stitch.

2 Make the handbag. From the blue felted wool, cut out a shape measuring 6 cm (2 in) in height, 4 cm (1½ in) in width at the top and 7 cm (2¾ in) at the bottom width.

3 Cut out two curved pieces for the flap, 4 cm (1½ in) in width – one in pale blue felt and the other in turquoise felt. Trim the blue piece so it is about 5 mm (¼ in) smaller along the curve. Glue the blue piece on top of the turquoise piece with the fabric glue and allow to dry.

4 Pin the sequin trim along the curve of the flap, next to the turquoise edge. Hand-sew in place with pink thread.

5 Using the yellow thread, sew the button on the centre bottom edge of the flap. Using yellow thread and a beading needle, sew the pink beads all over the front of the flap, using two stitches per bead and knotting securely. Sew a bugle bead on each side of the flap.

6 Glue the flap on top of the handbag shape with the fabric glue and leave to dry. Glue or stitch the length of pink cord along the top edge of the flap.

7 To make the handle, stitch the ends of the orange cord on the back of the handbag at each outermost side, using an overhand stitch (see page 143).

8 Pin and hand-sew the handbag to the scarf, using a decorative stitch like a blanket stitch around the edge.

Sequinned
Flower Hat

TRANSFORM A SIMPLE WOOLLY HAT into something reminiscent of a 1920s flapper. Certain to lift spirits, it will add a flash of glamour among all the dull neutral tones worn by others in the depths of winter. This plum colour will look great on blondes and brunettes alike. A longer, gently curved motif is the best choice, as it gives a 'sweep' of decoration. Don't choose a design that is too small or geometric in shape – it needs to have some curves.

WHAT YOU NEED
· Burgundy wool hat
· Ready-made burgundy sequin floral motif
· Deep wine-coloured thread
· Sewing needle

HOW TO DO IT

1 Pin the ready-made sequin motif in place on the hat. Try the hat on to check whether the positioning is correct. The motif will look best when it frames the face on one side.

2 Hand-sew the motif in place using slipstitch (see page 143). To anchor the knot, sew a few stitches into the wool and tie the ends in a knot before sewing and when finishing off the thread. Take care to work slowly and evenly so the hat does not stretch out of shape while you work.

Pink Net
and PVC Bag

Take the edge off high-sheen PVC with a frill of colourful spotted net and transform an inexpensive bag into an original one-of-a-kind. The contrast of textures and colours works to create a bag that is hardcore, yet undeniably feminine. For a night out, wear it with knee-high black patent boots and a devil-may-care attitude that hints at serious seductive powers.

WHAT YOU NEED

- Black PVC handbag
- Tape measure
- Pink spotted netting
- Scissors
- Pins
- Sewing machine
- Pink and black thread
- 15 mm-($\frac{5}{8}$ in-) wide black satin ribbon

HOW TO DO IT

1 Measure the circumference of the rim on the black bag. Cut a length of pink net three times this measurement. Decide on the depth of the frill and cut it to size. Here an 8 cm- ($3\frac{1}{4}$ in-) deep frill has been used on a 32 x 24 cm (12 $\frac{1}{2}$ x 9$\frac{1}{2}$ in) bag.

2 Fold and pin under the short ends of the net. Fold even, equally spaced pleats along the length of the net, pinning them in place. Check the length by holding the net along the edge of the top opening of the bag. Adjust the pleats and trim the net, if necessary, to achieve the correct length (see page 140).

3 Begin to machine-stitch the net onto the bag. Line the net up with one side seam and about 1 cm ($\frac{1}{2}$ in) below the top opening. Holding the net in your hand, machine-stitch the net to the bag. Work the entire way round the rim, removing the pins as you go.

4 Cut a length of black ribbon measuring 2.5 cm (1 in) more than the circumference of the bag. Pin to the edge of the bag to cover the pink net seam, turning under the short raw edge at the join. Using black thread, machine-stitch down both long sides to finish.

Studded Orange Belt

WHY SPEND A FORTUNE on a Marc by Marc Jacobs' rainbow belt when you can decorate a simple webbed belt with colourful studs? Orange is a hot vibrant colour, and one massively popular in the 1970s. The studs can be worked evenly in a row or at different heights for a more visually interesting effect. For example, keep all the studs at the same level except for coloured gemstone studs, or smaller studs, which 'break out' of line. For a wild zing of colour, wear the belt with a dark denim skirt or jeans.

WHAT YOU NEED
• Orange webbed belt
• A selection of gemstone and metal studs in assorted colours
• Chalk or pen fabric marker

1 On a flat work surface, arrange the studs in a row, moving them around to alternate shapes and colours.

2 When you have decided the order in which you want them, use the fabric marker to mark out dots on the belt where you want to insert the studs. Make sure the points are evenly spaced, but remember, some of the studs are bigger than others, so you will need to allow more space around them.

3 Following the manufacturer's instructions, press the first stud firmly into the fabric at the mark. On the reverse side, bend back the prongs with your finger or a metal teaspoon to secure the stud.

4 For gemstone studs, push the pronged piece through the belt from the wrong side at the marked position. Insert the stone into the centre and bend the prongs around the stone with a finger or a metal teaspoon to secure it.

5 Continue steps 3 and 4, as necessary, to insert all the gemstone and metal studs.

Glitzy Beret

WHO NEEDS PARIS? Berets look chic and stylish wherever you go. Their simple shape allows endless possibilities when it comes to customizing. You could try a post-Punk design with red sequins, safety pins and tiny badges on a black beret, or go for the urban military look with gold cord and brass buttons on Army green.

WHAT YOU NEED

- Moss green wool beret
- Assorted sequins in different shapes and colours
- Chalk or pen fabric marker (optional)
- Clear 'invisible' thread
- Beading needle

HOW TO DO IT

1 Place your sequins and decorations on a flat work surface and decide which ones work well together. Use flat beads in a mixture of different shapes and colours, as here, or try a same-colour theme but with sequins in various shapes and textures. Discard the ones that don't work with the others.

2 If desired, mark a dot at the point where you want to position each sequin with the fabric marker.

3 Hand-sew the sequins all over the beret. To do this, first make a knot in the invisible thread, and then bring the needle through to the right side of the beret. Secure each sequin with 2–3 stitches. For centrally positioned holes, make two stitches at opposite sides of the sequin.

Tropical
Flower Flip-flops

PINK SILK FLIP-FLOPS with black velvet thongs are used here for an exotic tropical look, but you could also decorate plain rubber flip-flops in the same way. Choose large plastic flowers in colours that complement your shoes. Whether you are wearing these for a summer garden party, to the beach or simply to a picnic in the park, they will lend a South Pacific feeling to the occasion. Wear them with a sarong, tiny T-shirt and vividly painted toenails.

WHAT YOU NEED
- A pair of silk and velvet flip-flops or plastic flip-flops
- 2 plastic flowers
- Super glue or a strong contact adhesive for plastics

HOW TO DO IT

1 Make sure the flip-flops are clean and dry.

2 Glue a flower to the front of the thong of each flip flop. To do this, coat both sides to be adhered, press firmly together so the glue can set, and then leave to dry. Follow the manufacturer's instructions for the glue. Some contact glues require you to mix two solvents, or to wait for a designated time before sticking the surfaces together.

Feather & Velvet
Slippers

LOW-HEELED PINK SATIN slippers with leopard print lining look extra-exotic when trimmed with turquoise feathers. This would look equally good on a pair of high-heels as a take on the marabou mule. Perfect for padding about your bedroom or for entertaining at home, these slippers should be seen and admired.

HOW TO DO IT

1 Measure the width of the front of the slipper where you want to attach the trim. Cut two strips of the feather trim to size. Cut two strips of velvet ribbon to size, plus an extra 1 cm (½in) on each one.

2 Using the hot glue gun, apply the glue along the rim of one slipper and immediately stick one piece of the feather trim in place. Hold for a few seconds, then leave to dry. Repeat with the other slipper.

3 Turn under and glue both short ends of each velvet ribbon by ½ cm (¼in). When dry, glue the velvet trim onto the edge of each slipper using the glue gun. Hold for a few seconds, then allow to dry.

4 To attach the gems, glue the reverse side and stick them on the velvet ribbon. Glue 10-12 gems on each shoe, equally spaced along the velvet trim.

WHAT YOU NEED
- Low-heeled fabric slippers
- Tape measure
- Turquoise feather trim
- Narrow lime velvet ribbon
- Scissors
- Hot glue gun (see page 142)
- 20-24 clear or turquoise flat-backed gemstones

Glitter Swirl Belt

THERE IS NO NEED TO GO ALL-OUT with military style if it is not your thing – just take a token accessory, like this Army-style webbed belt, and add a bit of girly glamour with glitter. Special fabric glitter, most often used for T-shirt decoration, is available from craft shops, specialist sewing shops, and the craft departments of large stores (see page 143). As a variation on this design, choose a glitter in the same colour as the belt, but highlight the pattern with gold or silver glitter. Because glitter can be tricky and a little unwieldy, use it with a more abstract motif; don't make the design too fussy or ornate. Try using script writing if your belt is wide enough – a simple word, like babe or foxy, looks good in curvy letters on the back of the belt.

WHAT YOU NEED

- Old newspapers
- Teal-blue webbed belt
- Cardboard or masking tape
- Chalk or pen fabric marker (optional)
- Fabric glue
- Fine washable fabric glitter in purple

1 Place newspaper on a work surface to help you clean up any spilled glitter later on. Either pin the belt to a length of cardboard or stick the ends to the work surface with masking tape so that the belt does not move around while you work.

2 Decide on the pattern you want to create. If you are unsure of working freehand, draw out your design on paper to the correct dimensions, and then copy it onto the belt using a chalk or pen fabric marker.

3 Practise squeezing out the fabric glue before you start; apply consistent pressure so that the glue comes out in a thin, even stream. Squeeze the fabric glue straight onto the belt to create the swirly pattern.

4 Sprinkle the purple glitter over the glue. There should be a heavy coating, without any glue showing through. Leave overnight to dry.

5 When dry, carefully shake off the excess glitter.

Gold-Splattered Denim Bag

THIS TAKE ON GLITZY GOLD uses Jackson Pollack-inspired splatters on a simple denim bag. If you really like this effect, try it on jeans (the colour works best against a dark denim background). You could try other colours too, but use only one colour of a metallic paint - you don't want to look as if you have been decorating your home. Practise first on paper if you are unsure of the effect you want to achieve. The long handle of the paintbrush will make the flicking technique easier to master.

WHAT YOU NEED

- Newspapers
- Plain dark denim bag
- Gold fabric paint
- 1 cm- (½ in-) wide artists' paintbrush, with a 25 cm (10 in) handle

HOW TO DO IT

1 Cover a large flat work surface with old newspapers. Place the denim bag, front side up, on the newspaper.

2 Dip the paintbrush into the gold paint and flick it over the bag in various directions, using a quick wrist action (see page 140). When you have applied enough splatters, leave the bag to dry.

3 Once the paint is dry, turn the bag over and apply the paint on the other side. Allow to dry.

Sequin Sneakers

WHAT YOU NEED

- Red canvas sneakers
- Super glue
- About 90 silver diamantes
- Tweezers
- Pink flat backed star gemstones

EVERYBODY'S BEEN GETTING into the trend for customizing their converses, so get out your favourite pair and give them a new lease of life. Merge comfort and style with these rhinestone-encrusted trainers - wearing them with bare legs and a short skirt is definitely a catwalk trend. For a variation on this, you could continue the rows of diamantes further down towards the toe of the shoe, or dot them about wherever you fancy. Add them to your heel or your front toe cap for a sparkly finish that is sure to turn heads.

HOW TO DO IT

1. Apply the glue in a thin stream along the side seams on one of the sneakers. Then, using a pair of tweezers, position the diamantes on the glue, working along the row. Glue them on one at a time and as close together as possible. Allow to dry.

2. Once the glue has dried, repeat step 1 to stick the diamante gems on the other side of the shoe. Repeat the process for the other sneaker.

Feather Hair Clips

WHAT YOU NEED

- Assorted feathers
- Scissors
- Short length of thin wire or adhesive tape
- 1 cm- (½ in-) wide velvet ribbon, measuring about 2.5 cm (1 in) long
- 4 flat-backed coloured gemstones
- Strong fabric glue
- Scissors
- Super glue or a hot glue gun
- Blank metal hair clip

ONCE THE UBIQUITOUS TRIM for hats, brooches and hair accessories, feathers are now enjoying a renaissance. Clipped into nape-of-neck chignons or just holding back hair above the ear, their gentle fringing effect frames the face and provides a contrast of texture to sleek shiny hair. You could try peacock feathers for the show off in you, ostrich plumes for some movie-star glamour, Native American-inspired browns and golds, or the multi-patterned feathers shown here.

HOW TO DO IT

1 Arrange the feathers to make an attractive bouquet. Use longer, thinner feathers underneath shorter, wider ones. Trim the quills and tie the ends with a short length of wire or adhesive tape.

2 Cut a length of velvet ribbon to secure the feathers. Apply fabric glue onto the wrong side of the ribbon. Remove the wire or tape from the quill ends and wrap the velvet around the ends of the feather bouquet, overlapping the ends on the underside.

3 Apply four drops of glue onto the velvet ribbon and stick on the gemstones, pressing in place to ensure they adhere. Allow to dry.

4 Open out the hair clip. Using a super glue or a hot glue gun, apply a thin stream of glue along the top of the clip. Line up the ribbon end of the feathers with the open end of the clip and stick it in place. If you are using a hot glue gun, the feathers will stick immediately to the clip; if using a super glue, you will need to hold the clip and feathers together until the glue begins to harden.

5 Leave the clip to dry overnight before wearing it.

How-to Techniques

Aany of the techniques described throughout the book can be employed with accessories. If you are concerned about committing a design to an item of clothing, begin with an inexpensive belt or bag. A layering of effects works well too; for example, embellish a bleached denim handbag with beading and flicks of metallic paint, or use glitter glue and studs on a belt.

ATTACHING NET FRILL

1 Pleat the net evenly, securing it with pins to the bag as you work. Adjust the pleats to fit the entire way round the bag, as necessary, and stitch in place using a running stitch.

FLICKING PAINT

1 Dip a long-handled artists' brush in the paint and then flick it onto the surface of the fabric using a quick wrist action. Intersperse flicks with long dribbles of paint. Allow to dry.

ATTACHING GEMSTONE AND DIAMANTÉ STUDS

1 Decide on the arrangement of the gemstones. If desired, mark the positions with a chalk or pen fabric marker.

2 Firmly press the stud clasp into the fabric from the reverse side, at the desired position, until the prongs emerge from the surface.

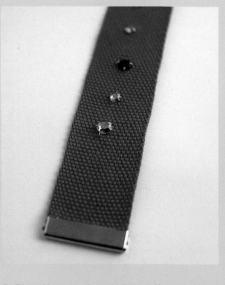

3 Place the gemstone between the prongs and bend the prongs over the stone with your thumb or a metal teaspoon to secure it.

Glossary

TOOLS

BEADING NEEDLE
A fine needle for sewing on beads that have very small holes.

CARDBOARD
Cardboard is available in various thicknesses and qualities. Use thicker card for inserting inside clothes when painting, bleaching or printing to avoid the paint or bleach going through to the other side of the fabric. Cardboard is also useful for hand-sewing, and as a substitute for a hoop for embroidery work to prevent stitching through to the other side of the fabric.

CHALK FABRIC MARKER
A chalk marker is useful for marking designs and measurements onto fabric, and it rubs or washes out. Some versions have a brush eraser at the end for removing the marks.

CRAFT KNIFE
A sharp cutting knife, such as a Stanley or X-Acto knife, should be used to cut out stencils. Alternatively use a thin-bladed scalpel, which is ideal for cutting out more intricately designed and curved shapes.

CUTTING MAT
A rubber mat which is used with a craft knife for cutting out stencils. It prevents the stencil from slipping and protects the work surface.

ELASTIC BANDS
Available in various sizes and thicknesses, the bands are used for tie-dying techniques.

EMBROIDERY HOOP
Wooden or plastic hoops that secure fabric and keep it taut for working decorative stitches.

GLUE GUN
This electrical tool enables instant glueing and will avoid the need for pressing or clamping pieces together until they are dry. To apply the glue, insert the special glue sticks, heat up the gun and press the trigger; the glue is released through the nozzle. Although the gun cannot be used on items you want to wash, it is ideal for adding gemstones, appliqués and trims to shoes and handbags or for attaching brooch pins to fake flowers.

IRON
An iron is essential for pressing clothes and ironing on transfers and heat-fusible webbing.

INVISIBLE OR FADE AWAY FABRIC MARKER
A special felt-tip pen used for marking fabric. The marks disappear with time.

NEEDLES
Available in a variety of sizes, specific needles are used with different types and weights of thread. Use sharps for hand-sewing, embroidery needles for stranded embroidery thread, and tapestry needles for tapestry wool or yarn.

PAINTBRUSHES
Owning a good range of different paintbrushes will enable you to create a huge variety of effects. Use large, medium and small house-decorating brushes for creating bold splashes of colour when fabric painting or bleaching. Use fine-tipped artists' brushes for detailed work and flicking paint or bleach. Always wash brushes thoroughly after use.

PINS
Use pins for temporarily securing together fabric, pinning up a hem or pinning on trimmings prior to sewing. Coloured-head pins are easier to see and remove than dressmaker's pins.

RULER
A transparent version allows you to see what you are measuring and enables you to line up letters or numbers horizontally. Any type of ruler is helpful when centring a design or for marking straight lines on fabric.

SCISSORS
Use sharp sewing scissors for cutting fabric and trims. Use embroidery scissors for cutting threads and trimmings, or for cutting out intricate appliqués. Use craft scissors for cutting paper or card. Do not use sewing scissors for cutting paper, as over time the blades will blunt.

SCREEN-PRINTING SCREEN
This is a basic wooden frame with a nylon mesh stretched over it. Screens can be purchased in a variety of sizes from craft suppliers or art shops.

SEWING MACHINE
A sewing machine enables you to create a variety of stitches, from straight and zigzag stitches to satin stitching or monogramming. Using a machine is a speedy way to attach trims and appliqués or to hem fabric.

SLEEVE BOARD
A small narrow board that clips onto an ironing board, a sleeve board is ideal for working on smaller areas, such as trouser legs or sleeves.

SQUEEGEE
A rubber-edged implement used for dragging paint across a screen-printing screen. You can substitute a thick piece of cardboard.

STENCIL BRUSH
This stubby brush with short bristles is essential for dabbing paint through a stencil. Use a larger size of brush, such as a 6, for large-scale designs, and a smaller size, such as a 4, for more detailed stencils.

STENCIL CARD
This is a professional paper made specifically for stencils. It is similar to thin cardboard, but waterproof, and it is available as plain cards for drawing onto and cutting out your own designs. Transparent stencil plastic is a useful alternative, but you will need to use an electric stencil cutter.

STENCILS
Pre-cut stencil designs are ready to use. They are usually cut out from a washable, reusable material, such as stencil card or acetate.

TAPE MEASURE
A flexible measuring tape that is essential for measuring fabric.

TWEEZERS
Use straight-edged cosmetic tweezers for picking up and positioning small gemstones.

MATERIALS

BEADS
Hundreds of different shapes, colours and textures of beads are available from craft shops, department stores or beading shops. Most of the beads used throughout the book are small round or straight glass beads.

BIAS BINDING
Binding is a strip of fabric cut on the bias. It is folded and pressed in such a way to create an encasing for neatly finishing the edges of fabrics and garments. You can cut your own from any fabric you like, but there are many colours and types of binding available which need only to be sewn in place.

BLEACH
This standard household fluid can be used to discolour and fade colour when it is applied onto natural fabrics and denims. Use caution when handling, as the bleach will discolour any fabric or furnishing onto which it splashes.

ELASTIC THREAD
A stretchy thread which is ideal for using on knits or stretchy fabrics, or for sewing on trim or beadwork that needs 'give'.

FABRIC DYE
Many brands and types are available, but they are usually sold as either for hand-dyeing or machine-dyeing. Refer to manufacturer's instructions before use, and make sure the dye is suitable for the fabric you are using.

FABRIC GLUE
This is a special adhesive used for glueing fabric shapes, trims or gemstones onto fabric. Always make sure the glue you use is

suitable for the materials. Using the same brand as the decoration will ensure the best possible adhesion. Glues specifically for use with washable glitter and sequins, and transfer foil are available.

FABRIC PAINT

This is a special paint that can be applied onto fabric. Once fixed, usually by ironing it on the reverse side of the design, it is fully washable. Read the manufacturer's advice for fabrics to use and fixing techniques.

FEATHER TRIM

Available in various colours and styles, feather trims are secured in a simple ribbon binding for stitching on. Often feather trims include beads or a decorative trim, and can be hand-sewn onto the right side of a garment.

FELT

This is a cloth made from pressed wool. You can buy squares of craft felt in a multitude of colours from craft or specialist sewing shops. It is easy to cut and does not fray. Felted wool is a thicker, more textured fabric than craft felt and can be purchased by the metre (yard) from sewing shops.

FUSIBLE WEBBING

This is a heat-reactive bonding agent that will hold an appliqué, trim or hem to fabric without stitching. It is available as a length of webbing, which needs to be inserted between two layers of fabric before ironing to fuse in place, or as a paper-backed variety, which can be fused onto one side of fabric before ironing it to the other. Read the manufacturer's recommendations for the correct fabric and the ironing technique.

GEMSTONE STUDS

These are metal clasps that have four prongs for holding gemstones. They are pressed through the wrong side of the fabric and a gemstone is inserted in the prongs. The prongs are then bent over the stone to hold it in place.

GEMSTONES OR DIAMANTES

These sparkly synthetic stones can be glued in place with fabric glue or a super glue. They can also be inserted into gemstone studs.

GLITTER FABRIC PAINT

This is a clear fabric paint containing fine glitter particles, available in a range of colours. When the paint is dry, the glitter sparkles.

IRON-ON EMBROIDERED MOTIFS OR TRANSFERS

Embroidered appliqués and pre-cut transfers have a heat-reactive webbing on the reverse side. The motifs can be positioned anywhere on a garment and ironed in place.

MACHINE-WASHABLE GLITTER

This super-fine glitter in a range of colours can only be applied to clothing with a special fabric glue made by the same company as the glitter. Read the manufacturer's instructions for application techniques.

MACHINE-WASHABLE TRANSFER FOIL

This is a decorative foil and can only be applied with a special fabric glue made by the same company as the foil. The transfer foil is available in a range of colours. Read the manufacturer's instructions for application techniques.

METAL STUDS

These are available in silver and gold metal and in different shapes and sizes. They have four prongs, which are inserted through the right side of the fabric. The prongs are then opened out and pressed flat on the reverse side of the fabric to hold the stud in place.

PUFFA PAINT

This is a heat-reactive paint, which can be applied directly to fabric to create a design. When the paint is dry, the design is turned wrong side out and ironed, at which point the paint starts to puff. Never iron the paint directly. Refer to the manufacturer's instructions.

RIBBON ROSES

These can be purchased ready-made. They can also be made by wrapping a short length of narrow ribbon into a rosette and securing the shape in place with a few stitches.

RIBBONS AND TRIMMINGS

An array of textures, colours, styles, patterns and widths are available, from velvet ribbon, sequin trim and fringing to lace, rickrack and cord. Many can be machine-stitched in place, however more delicate lace and beadwork will need to be hand-sewn.

SEQUINS

Loose sequins have tiny holes that allow them to be stitched in place individually. Sequins are also available without holes, and these are glued on with strong fabric glue. Sequin trim is a decorative length of small round sequins held together with thread, which can be hand-sewn or machine-stitched in place.

SUPER GLUE OR CONTACT GLUE

A very strong contact glue that immediately bonds materials together. Read the manufacturer's advice for materials that can be bonded and always follow the application instructions. These types of glue should not be used on clothing.

THREADS

General-purpose cotton or polyester thread is used for hand-sewing and machine-stitching. Stranded cotton embroidery thread (floss) is used for decorative stitching; usually this is available six-stranded and the strands can be separated for finer work. Tapestry wool or yarn is much thicker than embroidery thread and is often used for embroidery work on heavier woollen garments.

TRANSFER PRINT

A coloured image is photocopied onto special transfer paper, which is then positioned onto a garment of fabric and transferred using a special press. The technique requires enlisting the help of a specialist copier or T-shirt printing shop.

SEWING STITCHES

BLANKET STITCH

This stitch is used to hem raw edges, or as decoration. Insert the needle through the fabric so that it points up to the top edge , wind the loose thread over the needle and pull it through the loop.

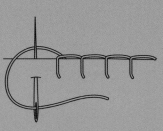

COUCH STITCH

If you are couching thread, insert it through the fabric and lay it along or around the shape. Do the same if you are couching cord, but don't insert it through the fabric. Thread another needle with a finer thread in the same or a contrasting colour, and sew even stitches across the thread/cord.

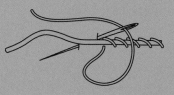

DAISY CHAIN STITCH

Bring the needle through the fabric where you want to start the chain and insert it back in just to the right of where the thread came through to create a small loop. Insert the needle back through the fabric about a stitch length to the left and bring it up and over the looped thread. Repeat to create subsequent loops.

Resources

FEATHER STITCH
This is a decorative loop stitch which is worked alternately from right and left of a given line, following the same principles as for the daisy chain stitch (see above).

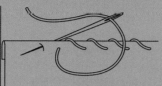

FRENCH KNOT
Tie a knot at the end of the thread and insert the needle through the reverse of the fabric. Wind the thread around the needle twice and insert it back through the fabric close to where it came up.

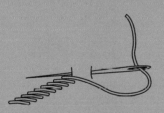

SEED STITCH
These are small, random stitches that can vary in length. Insert the needle through the reverse of the fabric and then back through at a distance to create the desired length of stitch.

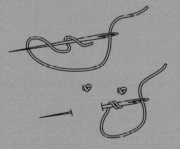

SLIP STITCH
This stitch is used to hem fabric. With the needle, sew into the folded hem fabric and catch a thread from the main fabric, spacing the stitches evenly apart.

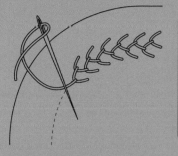

STEM STITCH
This stitch is used to outline a marked design; altering the angle of the stitch will vary the width of the stitched line. Insert the needle through the fabric and make the first stitch. Make the next stitch next door to the first, and so on, keeping the stitches even.

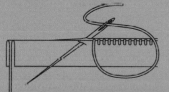

OVERHAND
These tiny, even stitches are used to join two finished edges – for example, attaching ribbon or lace edging to a garment. Insert the needle diagonally from the back edge through to the front, picking up only one or two threads each time. Insert the needle directly behind the thread from the previous stitch and bring it out a stitch length away.

FW BRAMWELL & CO. LTD
Old Empress Mills
Empress Street
Colne, Lancs BB8 9HU
01232 860388
www.bramwellcrafts.co.uk
Glitter, foils, fabric glue and paint.

DOVER BOOKSHOP
18 Earlham Street
London WC2H 9LG
020 78362111
www.doverbooks.co.uk

DYLON INTERNATIONAL LTD
Worsley Bridge Road
London SE26 5HD
Advice line: 020 8663 4296
www.dylon.co.uk
Fabric dyes, paints and pens.

ELLS & FARRIER
20 Beak Street
London W1F 9RE
020 76299964
www.creativebeadcraft.co.uk
Beads, gemstones and studs.

THE ENGLISH STAMP COMPANY
Worth Matravers
Dorset BH19 3JP
01929 439117
www.englishstamp.com
Rubber stamps and fabric paint.

HOMECRAFTS DIRECT
PO Box 38
Leicester LE1 9BU
0845 458 4532
Screen-printing equipment.

THE STENCIL LIBRARY
Stocksfield Hall
Stocksfield
Northumberland NE43 7TN
01661 844844
www.stencil-library.com
Stencils in all sorts of designs.

Acknowledgements
Thanks to the following for props:

ANDREW MARTIN (wallpapers)
200 Walton Street
London SW3 2JL
020 7225 5100

CATH KIDSTON
8 Clarendon Cross
London W11 4AP
020 7221 4000
www.cathkidston.co.uk

JACQUELINE EDGE
1 Courtnell Street
London W2 5BU
020 7229 1172
www.jacquelineedge.com

MUJI
Whiteleys Shopping Centre
London W2 4YN
Mail order: 020 7792 8283

THE PAINT LIBARY
5 Elystan Street
London SW3 3NT
020 7823 7755
www.paintlibary.co.uk

PAPERCHASE
213 Tottenham Court Road
London W1T 9PS
020 7467 6200
www.paperchase.co.uk

SANDERSONS
Sanderson House
Oxford Road
Denham, Bucks UB9 4DX
www.sanderson-online.com

Thanks to the following for their customizing contributions:
Nancy Bridgewater, Katy Hackney, Claire Kitchener, Kim Robertson, Emma Eardley.

Index